American
Red Cross

StayWell®

W9-BRX-075

American Red Cross Babysitter's Training Handbook

The following organizations provided review of the materials and/or support for the American Red Cross Babysitter's Training program:

AAPCC   Girl Scouts®   jcc association   NMSA.

Content reflects the 2005 Consensus on Science for CPR and Emergency Cardiovascular Care (ECC) and the 2005 Guidelines for First Aid.

American Red Cross certificates may be issued upon successful completion of a training program, which uses this manual as an integral part of a course. By itself, the material in this handbook does not constitute comprehensive Red Cross training. In order to issue Red Cross certificates, your instructor must be authorized by the American Red Cross, and must follow prescribed policies and procedures. Make certain that you have attended a course authorized by the Red Cross. Contact your local American Red Cross chapter (*www.redcross.org*) for more information.

The emergency care procedures outlined in this manual reflect the standard of knowledge and accepted emergency practices in the United States at the time this manual was published. It is the reader's responsibility to stay informed of changes in the emergency care procedures.

Printed in the United States of America
Printing/Binding by RR Donnelly

StayWell
780 Township Line Rd.
Yardley, PA 19067

ISBN: 978-1-58480-426-0

08 09 10 11 12 9 8 7 6 5 4 3 2 1

Acknowledgments

The American Red Cross Babysitter's Training program and supporting materials were developed through the dedication of both employees and volunteers. Their commitment to excellence made this program possible.

The American Red Cross and StayWell thank Kristin Atwell, Michael Atwell, David Baker, Elina Berglund, Charles Boyce Brooks III, Juliet Chukwu, Meghan Gordineer, Julionna Hackett, Kylee Anne Hackett, Audrey Heller, Anne Mammel, Ashley Radley, Juliana Saucedo and Natalie Scalabrino for their guidance and review. The American Red Cross and StayWell also thank Vincent Knaus, photographer, and Tamara Lazarus, producer, for their efforts.

American Red Cross' Advisory Council on First Aid, Aquatics, Safety and Preparedness
In late 1998, the Red Cross formed an independent panel of nationally recognized health and safety experts known as the Advisory Council on First Aid, Aquatics, Safety and Preparedness or ACFASP. Drawing on a body of collective expertise from such diverse fields as emergency medicine, occupational health, sports medicine, school health, emergency medical services (EMS) response and disaster mobilization, ACFASP helps establish the standard in first aid care. ACFASP advises the Red Cross in areas related to the development and dissemination of audience-appropriate information and training in first aid, aquatics, safety and preparedness.

Contents

CHAPTER 1

You're the Boss: A Guide to Leadership

Babysitting is a big responsibility. Are you ready for the challenge?

What happens if the kids don't listen when you tell them it is time for bed? What will you do if a stranger comes to the door? How will you handle fighting or temper tantrums? As the babysitter, you're the leader. Parents rely on you to keep their children safe when they are away. Children look up to you as the person in charge. In this chapter, you will learn the leadership skills you will need to meet these challenges.

How to be a Leader

A leader is a person who guides and motivates others towards a common goal. In babysitting, the people you'll be motivating will be the children in your care. The common goal will be keeping everyone safe, respecting the family's rules and routines and having fun.

There are a lot of ways to lead children and some babysitters may find that some leadership styles are more natural for them than others. You may not remember the names of the styles and that's okay; knowing how and when to use each leadership style will help you while you're on the job. In most cases, the leadership style that you use will depend on the circumstances.

If the kids you are babysitting are trying to make a decision that affects everyone but doesn't involve safety, it's best to use a **democratic leadership style**. For example, if the children can't decide whether to go to the park or watch a DVD, don't immediately decide for them. Instead, ask each child to say what he or she prefers to do and try to work through the decision together. Try to keep the discussion positive. This approach allows each child to feel like his or her opinions are listened to and respected.

If the children are getting along very well and no important decisions need to be made, you can probably use a **hands-off leadership style.** For example, if three sisters have been playing a board game without any conflicts and a slight disagreement comes up, you don't need to step in. In a case like this, you can just let the girls work things out on their own. Using the hands-off leadership style can keep you from seeming too bossy and it gives the children an opportunity to learn how to solve disagreements on their own. If the conflict gets worse or the children can't resolve the problem themselves, then it's time for you to step in and take action.

When you are just getting to know the children or when emotions are running high, the **sympathetic leadership style** works well. A sympathetic leader focuses on making people feel valued and cared for. This style works best in situations where it is more important to focus on how people feel than on how they are acting, like when you are babysitting a brother and sister who both want your attention. If they are safe and not hurting each other, then take your time and listen to what each child has to say and ignore their minor attention-seeking behavior. By focusing on the children's feelings and taking the time to listen to their concerns, you can earn their trust.

Sometimes a babysitter needs to make an important decision quickly and has to tell the children what to do with little or no discussion. You will need to use the **directive leadership style** in emergencies and when you are trying to prevent an injury. For example, if one child is about to hit another child with a stick, you must tell the child to stop and take the stick away. You don't have time to discuss the situation because immediate action is needed.

Leadership Skills

Everyone can learn to be a leader. As with other skills, the more you practice leadership skills, the better leader you will be. Practice the following to improve your leadership skills:

- Role modeling
- Respect
- Communication
- Motivation
- Taking action
- Decision making

Role Modeling

A role model sets an example for others to follow. Modeling good behavior is important because the children you babysit will look up to you and follow the example you set. Role modeling is also one of the simplest ways to lead. For example, always washing your hands before preparing or eating food will help you encourage the children to wash their hands. You can be a good role model by—

- Following household rules.
- Following the parent's instructions.
- Having a positive attitude.
- Making the best out of difficult situations.
- Leading by example.
- Focusing on safety.
- Showing enthusiasm.

Respect

Respecting Household Rules

An important part of being a good leader is knowing what is expected of you. The parents for whom you babysit will have specific instructions for how they want you to handle certain situations. Respect and follow all the household rules, even if they are different from your own. The children will be happier, feel more secure and behave better if you follow their usual routines.

Respecting Diversity

People are alike in many ways. In other ways, people are very different. These differences are called diversity. Diversity is a good thing. Without diversity, everyone would be exactly the same and that would make the world a very boring place. Accept each child as someone special. Being respectful of other's diversity also means recognizing how your own culture and beliefs might affect how you get along with children who are different from you. Respecting diversity is a great way to model respect and courtesy and will help you become a better communicator. Respect each family's and child's diversity. You may find that the children you babysit are diverse in the following ways:

- **Age and developmental stage**. Even though children typically go through certain stages and reach different milestones at predictable ages, many children act in different ways, even at the same age and stage.

- **Gender.** While boys and girls are physically different and tend to have some different interests, don't assume that *all* boys or *all* girls act a certain way or like the same things. Some girls may enjoy playing with cars and climbing trees while others don't. Some boys may not like to play sports. Also, keep in mind that there are many activities, such as reading books and playing games, that most kids like to do regardless of their gender.

- **Temperament.** Kids can vary in their responses to the same situation. Some do not seem bothered by anything, while others become upset or cry very easily.

○ **Cultural differences.** If you babysit for a child whose family is from a different country or culture than your own, the family might speak with an accent, look different than you or dress in clothes that are unfamiliar. They might have different customs and ways of doing things. You can learn a lot from these families—all about new foods, customs and holidays. This is also a fun way to learn new words.

○ **Religious beliefs.** You may care for kids with religious beliefs different from your own. The parents might give special instructions, such as "Make sure Johnnie says his prayers" or "Make sure Suzy doesn't eat meat."

○ **Family members.** You might care for children living with one parent, a step-parent, a guardian or other relatives who are not the child's parents.

○ **Children with special needs.** Some children with special needs may use equipment, like a wheelchair, or may not be able to eat certain foods because they are allergic. If you care for children who have special needs, then it's very important to follow their parent's instructions. Remember to be patient with them; their bodies and minds may work differently from yours.

○ **Family income.** All families do not have the same amount of money to spend and every family is different in how they choose to spend their money. The children you babysit will have different kinds of toys and clothes and live in different homes and neighborhoods. Children can grow up happy and healthy no matter how much the family spends on clothes, toys, food and other things.

Communication
Communicating with Children

It is especially important for babysitters to know how to talk and listen to children. Remember the following when you're speaking with children:

○ **Keep it simple.**

   ○ Use short sentences and words the child understands to avoid confusion.

○ **Keep it positive.**

   ○ Tell the kids what you want them to do instead of what they shouldn't do. For example, say, "Please put your plate in the sink" instead of, "Don't leave your plate on the table."

   ○ Give the child reasonable choices between acceptable options. For example, if you want to ask the child what he or she wants to drink you could say, "Would you like milk or water?"

○ **Be specific.**

   ○ Tell children exactly what you like or don't like about what they are doing. For example, if you like it when Lucy picks up her toys, say, "I like it when you pick up your toys" rather than, "You're a good girl." If you don't like it when Danny throws his blocks, say, "I do not like it when you throw your blocks" rather than, "You are a bad boy."

   ○ Kids can also have a hard time understanding how their behaviors influence others, so it is important to tell children how their actions affect you and others. For example, you might say, "When you throw your blocks, it scares me because you might hurt yourself or somebody else."

○ **Show courtesy and respect.**

   ○ Say "please" and "thank you."

   ○ Don't call children names or insult them. Insults and name calling cause hurt feelings and neither will help the kids to understand what they have done wrong.

   ○ Showing courtesy and respect will help you establish good relationships with children and be a better leader.

○ **Stay calm.**

   ○ Speak in a calm voice when disciplining, even if you are upset or angry. If a child is yelling or screaming, say, "I can't understand you when you yell," or, "You need to tell me why you are upset so that I can help."

   ○ Use humor when things are tense. For example, if a child is having a hard time getting over being upset, you can try acting goofy or using a joke to lighten the mood, but do not make fun of the child.

○ **Show you are listening.**

   ○ If you cannot do what the child wants right away, let him or her know you are listening and have heard the request. For example, if a child wants to go to the park and you need to ask his or her parent or guardian first, explain this to the child. Children will not feel ignored if you show them that you are listening.

   ○ Sit down or kneel so that you are at the child's eye level.

   ○ Make eye contact.

   ○ Ask questions to make sure you understand what a child is saying.

   ○ Show genuine interest in the children you are babysitting.

Communicating with Adults

A good babysitter should also be able to communicate with adults. The way you speak with parents can highlight your leadership skills and increase the chances that they will hire you. When talking to adults, follow these guidelines:

- **Be positive.** Show enthusiasm for your job. If you ever have to talk to parents about an issue with their children, make sure you also mention positive things.

- **Be specific.** For example, tell them the exact times and dates you can work. Avoid using unspecific words such as "about," "around" or "like."

- **Be honest.** Tell the truth.

- **Be polite.** Treat parents with courtesy and respect.

Motivation

A leader uses motivation to get others to follow him or her. Below are some ways you can motivate the children you babysit.

- **Give positive feedback.** Let the children know if they are behaving well and recognize their efforts. Give positive feedback often. The children will feel good about themselves and be more likely to behave. If the children misbehave, then use corrective feedback to stop or change how they are acting. Corrective feedback means telling children what to do instead of what they did wrong.

- **Be original.** Use creativity when you run into problems. Treat each babysitting job individually. Try not to fall into routines.

- **Have purpose.** Come to each babysitting job prepared. Plan out activities ahead of time. Think about what rules and boundaries you will set. Clearly state your expectations. Bring extra supplies and have a back-up plan ready in case things change.

- **Be flexible.** A good leader also knows how to go with the flow. As long as things are safe and you follow the household rules, then it is okay to change plans.

- **Encourage cooperation.** When possible, try to include the children in decision making. For example, if there is a choice between playtime activities, ask the children what they want to do. Remember, it is the babysitter's job to make all the important decisions.

Taking Action

People look to leaders to take action when no one else will. In difficult situations it is easy to think that someone else will handle things or that solving the problem is not your responsibility. But if no one takes responsibility, then no one will act. A leader will risk sounding foolish or standing out to make the right choice in a difficult situation. There are three steps to taking action:

1. **Notice that action is needed.** Be alert for any changes in the children's behavior or your situation that might lead to problems. For example, are the children outside and it's beginning to rain or have they started playing too aggressively?

2. **Take responsibility.** Ask yourself if action is needed and then take responsibility for the situation.

3. **Act.** Don't worry about looking foolish or standing out and take action to fix the situation. Remember, only do what you are trained to do and what you can do safely.

Decision Making

As a babysitter, you might have to decide how to handle a challenging situation on your own. This is the main reason parents hired you. Parents rely on you to make good decisions when they can't. When you are faced with a tough situation, use the FIND decision-making model to help you decide what to do.

FIND Decision-Making Model

Step 1 **Figure out the problem.**
- Focus on the exact problem that is causing trouble.

Step 2 **Identify possible solutions.**
- Think about all the possible ways you could solve the problem.

Step 3 **Name pros and cons for each solution.**
- Think about the positive and negative consequences of each way to solve the problem.

Step 4 **Decide which solution is best, then act on it.**
- Decide which solution is best, then take action.

CHILD ABUSE AND NEGLECT

Child abuse is the term for hurting a child physically, emotionally or sexually. Child neglect is the failure to provide for the child's basic needs. Some indications of child abuse and neglect include—

- Unexplained bruises, burns or scars. Often, physically abused children are afraid of contact, such as hugging or being held.

- Having low self-esteem, being very sad or crying a lot, acting quiet or being very loud and aggressive.

- Fear of undressing or having physical contact with anyone. The child may have signs of sexual abuse or physical abuse.

- Being left alone for long periods of time or in dangerous situations. Some neglected children may be dressed in improper or worn-out clothing, display a lack of cleanliness or are overly concerned with cleanliness and may beg or steal food or money.

All kids get bruises and sometimes are sad or cry, but if you notice these signs continuing over time, the child might be abused. If you think a child in your care has been abused, then how you act is important. Your actions can protect the child. Tell an adult you trust, like your parent or guardian or a teacher, about your concerns and ask him or her for help. If you are unsure, you can talk to a professional crisis counselor 24 hours a day, 7 days a week by calling the Childhelp National Child Abuse Hotline at 1-800-4-A-CHILD (1-800-422-4453). Call the police if you feel that the situation is life threatening.

Desert Island

Directions: *Working in your groups, rank each of the following items in order of importance for survival on a desert island (rank from 1 most important to 7 least important).*

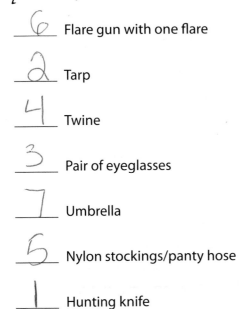

___6___ Flare gun with one flare

___2___ Tarp

___4___ Twine

___3___ Pair of eyeglasses

___7___ Umbrella

___5___ Nylon stockings/panty hose

___1___ Hunting knife

FIND Decision-Making Model Activity

Directions: Practice using the FIND decision-making model by filling in the blanks below after watching the scenario.

Restless Ronald

F

Figure out the problem.

The little boy Roland wont
got to bed

I

Identify possible solutions.

you could tell him to go
to bed and if he say no
again give him time out I
be com about it

N

Name pros and cons for each solution.

+ call the parents
+ Read him another bed time
story and force him to go
to bed
- or just give in

know _____ for _____
_____ bed at _____

D

Decide which solution is best, then act on it.

The Best soultion is to bed
and say no

CHAPTER 2

The Business of Babysitting

What kind of babysitter are you?

Will you work on school nights? How many children will you babysit? How much will you charge? Are you willing to prepare dinner? As a babysitter, you will have to be able to answer these and many other questions. Babysitting is a very big responsibility. When families hire you, they are entrusting you with the care of their children and their homes. They want a strong leader who enjoys children and will keep them safe.

Families also want someone who is reliable. It doesn't matter if you are the best babysitter in the world—if you are late or cancel appointments all the time, then you won't receive job offers. Parents want to hire babysitters who take their jobs seriously—babysitters who act professionally from start to finish.

This chapter is designed to help you learn the business of babysitting, which is the key to a successful babysitting career. From finding babysitting jobs to figuring out how much to charge, this chapter will help you become the kind of babysitter who is asked to babysit again and again.

Getting Started

Ask Your Parents

Before beginning your career as a babysitter, talk to your parents. They will have rules and expectations about when, where, how often and for whom you can babysit. The first step to becoming a safe and successful babysitter is to know your own family's expectations.

There may also be state or local laws governing how old you must be to babysit and the number of hours or children you are allowed to babysit. Ask your course instructor or contact your State Attorney General's Office, local child welfare department, local department of human services or local child protective services for information on the laws in your area.

Assessing Your Skills

The next step to becoming a safe and successful babysitter is assessing your babysitting skills. Just as science teachers are different than English teachers, babysitters differ from one another. For example, one babysitter may be especially good at crafts while another babysitter may have experience taking care of infants. Every babysitting job is different as well. Some jobs may require special skills or extra experience, such as babysitting for infants, several young children at the same time, children with special needs or when babysitting at night or for several hours. Do not accept jobs that are beyond your abilities. Use the Babysitter's Self-Assessment Tool on the *Babysitter's Training CD-ROM* or on *www.redcross.org* to determine your skills, abilities and interests. Update the Babysitter's Self-Assessment Tool about every 6 months.

Finding Work

The best business comes through word of mouth. Parents would rather hire a babysitter they know, but the next best thing would be to hire a babysitter recommended by someone they trust.

One of the best ways to get babysitting jobs is by networking. Ask parents to ask friends, relatives and neighbors if they need a babysitter or if they know someone else who does. Talk to other babysitters and offer to fill in as a substitute.

THINGS TO DISCUSS WITH YOUR PARENTS

Before starting out as a babysitter ask your parents these questions:

- When am I allowed to babysit?
- How often can I babysit?
- For whom can I babysit?
- How many children may I babysit at one time?
- What are your rules and expectations for me as a babysitter?

Before accepting any babysitting job, ask your parents for permission. Each time you leave to babysit, be sure to—

- Give your parents the phone number and address for your babysitting job.
- Let your parents know all the details of your babysitting job (e.g., how many hours you will be gone or if you plan to leave the house with the kids).
- Remind your parents that you will call before you leave the job so they will know when to expect you home. Let them know if the job is running late.
- Arrange check-in times and transportation home with your parents, if needed.
- Agree on a code word to use in a phone call home if you feel unsafe or threatened. For example, if a family member has offered to drive you home but you suspect he or she may have been drinking, call your parents and use the code word so they would know to come pick you up.

Business cards can be a very helpful tool for building up your babysitting business. You can make your own business cards using the templates found on the *Babysitter's Training CD-ROM*. Give your business cards to families interested in hiring you. Ask friends, relatives and neighbors to give your cards to people they know who might need a babysitter.

It is alright for you to give out your business cards to people you know and trust and to ask them to distribute your cards to people they know, but you should not advertise to the general public. DO NOT POST YOUR NAME, ADDRESS AND/OR PHONE NUMBER ON THE INTERNET. DO NOT PLACE YOUR BUSINESS CARDS OR FLIERS IN COFFEE SHOPS, SUPERMARKETS OR OTHER PUBLIC PLACES. It is unsafe to allow total strangers to get your name, address, phone number or even e-mail addresses.

If your networking results in job offers from families you don't know, be sure to talk to your parents. Whether or not you should accept a job from a stranger is an important decision that your parents should help you make.

MOTHER'S HELPERS

Working as a mother's helper is another way to use your babysitter's training. A mother's helper assists with child care while a parent is at home. Additional duties sometimes include light housework, preparing simple meals and/or cleaning up.

Families that home school, have at least one parent who works from home, have more than two children or have a stay-at-home parent often hire mother's helpers. Mother's helpers usually get work on a regular basis because these families need their help routinely.

While mother's helpers usually are paid for their work, volunteering for this job is a good way for inexperienced or younger babysitters to gain experience. Just as you would with a babysitting job, make sure you talk with your parents about their expectations for you as a mother's helper before accepting any jobs.

Resume

A resume is another great tool for helping you get babysitting jobs. A resume is a brief summary of your skills, qualifications and experience along with some personal information. You should have a resume ready to give to families interested in hiring you as their babysitter.

A babysitter's resume should list your name, address, phone number, e-mail address and school, as well as work experience, skills and abilities. It should also include the names and phone numbers of families you have babysat for in the past, who were satisfied with your work and who have agreed to serve as references. If you are just starting out, you can use teachers, coaches or other adults who know you well as references. Make sure anyone who has agreed to serve as a reference knows that you have put them on your resume and understands that they may get phone calls asking for a reference about you.

Update your resume frequently. You can build your own resume using the template on the *Babysitter's Training CD-ROM*. For an example, see the babysitting resume on page 18 (Fig. 2-1). Remember, do not post your resume in public places.

Money, Money, Money

The next thing you need to do before you get started in the business of babysitting is to figure out how much to charge. After all, this is the reason why many get started babysitting in the first place. Sometimes parents will offer you a specific rate. At other times it will be up to you. When you meet with a new family, you should be prepared to answer the question, "How much do you charge?"

Be fair when setting your hourly rate. Talk to other babysitters in your area and find out what they are charging. You can also ask other parents how much they have paid babysitters in the past. Sometimes babysitters charge more for additional children or extra duties, such as cleaning and/or cooking.

Make sure to discuss your rate and payment details before accepting any babysitting job. Tell the family if you prefer to be paid in cash or if you will accept checks. If the parents don't mention the rate, you can politely tell them what you charge. For example, you could say, "Thank you for this opportunity Mr. and Mrs. Chilton. Before accepting the job I'd like to discuss my rate. I usually charge $___ an hour. Is that okay with you?"

It's okay if a parent tries to negotiate a different rate with you; just remember that you can negotiate too. Figure out in advance how low you are willing to go. If a parent tries to bargain for a lower rate, you can counter with a different rate until you and the family reach an agreement.

FIGURE 2-1

Karen Sitter

1234 Safety Street   karensitter@email.abc
Golden Valley, MN 00001   (111)555-6666

EDUCATION

    Pleasant Elementary School

    6th Grade

    Family and Consumer Science - honors class, honor roll 4th and 5th grade

TRAINING

    American Red Cross Babysitter's Training Course

    Leadership, professionalism, safety, child development, basic child care and care for emergencies

ADDITIONAL TRAINING

    American Red Cross First Aid

    American Red Cross CPR—Child and Infant

BABYSITTING EXPERIENCE

    The Tunney's   09/10/07

    Babysat for two children ages 3 and 7 for 3 hours

    Prepared dinner and put the children to bed

    Helped older child get started on homework

    The Oaksmiths's   08/02/07

    Babysat one child with special needs, age 4, for 4 hours

Interviewing the Family

Assessing the Job and Gathering Information

Not all babysitting jobs are the same. Babysitting a well-behaved 7 year old on a school night is quite different from babysitting two rowdy toddlers on a Saturday afternoon. Some families may ask you to make dinner or give their children a bath. Others may ask you to babysit well past your curfew. This is why it's important to always interview the family before taking any babysitting job. An interview is the best way for families to find out if you are right for the babysitting job and for you to find out if the job is right for you.

Come to the interview prepared. Bring along copies of the Family Interview Form and Parental Consent and Contact Form, which can be found on the *Babysitter's Training CD-ROM*. Be sure to read through these forms before you get to the interview. Use both forms for each new babysitting job. Even if you have babysat for a family before, you still need to assess the job and update any new information. Also, bring copies of your resume and references and use a clipboard or file folder to keep your paperwork organized.

Your main goal during an interview should be to assess the job and gather detailed information. Compare the job details with your babysitting skills, availability, expectations and preferences, as well as with the expectations of your parents. Be certain to meet the children you will be babysitting. Even if you really like the family or want the money, you should never take on a babysitting job that exceeds your abilities or one that you are uncomfortable with for any other reason. Likewise, you may not be able to take a job if you have homework to do or have plans with your friends.

Covering the following points will help you assess the job:

- **Date.** Find out the date of the job. Be sure to check your schedule for conflicts and ask your parents before accepting any babysitting jobs.

- **Transportation.** How will you get to and from the job? Never walk home alone at night. Always get approval from your parents for your transportation arrangements.

- **Number of children.** Do not offer to babysit for more children than you can safely handle. For most babysitters, that means no more than three children. Use your self-assessment form and talk to your parents about how many kids they feel you can handle. If there are too many children for you to safely babysit, ask if you can bring along another babysitter to help. Make sure the other babysitter meets the family before the job and you discuss payment and the job details with them. If you have a friend babysit with you, remember your focus should be on the kids you are babysitting, not each other.

- **Ages of children.** In general, younger children need more care. Babysitting jobs where you are expected to watch several young children (three or more) by yourself can be very challenging. Do not accept these types if you do not feel comfortable doing so. New babysitters should not babysit infants or more than one toddler until they have some experience.

- **Length of time.** Long hours make the job harder and may interfere with your homework, activities or free time. If you are new to babysitting, you might want to start out with short shifts (1–2 hours).

- **Time of day.** Watching children at night when they are sleeping is easier than watching them during the day. Some parents may stay out late; make sure you find out when they plan to be home.

Also, find out the following details:

- **Responsibilities.** Some families may ask you to do other chores like bathing a child or preparing meals. Do not accept any additional responsibilities unless you are willing and can do them safely.

- **House rules.** Know the house rules for both yourself and the children. For example, it is better to know if children are allowed to play certain video games or have dessert after dinner before they tell you, "My mommy said I can!"

- **Children with special needs.** Some children with special needs may use equipment, like a wheelchair. Before babysitting a child with special needs make sure you learn the specific duties, tasks and responsibilities to care for that child and determine if you are capable of meeting his or her needs while babysitting. You do not have to accept a babysitting job if you do not feel comfortable performing any of the care duties, tasks or responsibilities that are expected of you.

- **Pets.** Find out if the family has any pets, if they are friendly and if you are expected to care for them.

HOW TO ACE AN INTERVIEW

- Arrive 10 minutes early.

- Dress appropriately. Brush your hair and make sure your hands and fingernails are clean. Wear neat, clean clothes.

- Bring copies of your resume, references and business cards. Be prepared to answer questions about your availability, but do not accept a job without your parents' permission.

- Be friendly and polite. Say "please" and "thank you." Maintain eye contact and nod your head to show that you are listening.

- Tell the family about yourself. Include your hobbies and interests. Be sure to mention activities such as scouting, youth groups, summer camps or sports from which you gained leadership skills.

- Show enthusiasm towards the family and the job. Don't just sit there quietly. Ask questions about duties and responsibilities. Ask if you can meet the children and try to get to know them. Make sure you wash your hands before playing with or holding children, especially infants.

- Be prepared and willing to talk about your babysitting abilities.

  - Talk about your experience including the—

    - Number and types of babysitting jobs you've had (include the children's ages and the hours you worked).

    - Babysitting activities you have planned.

    - Babysitting situations you have handled.

    - Volunteer and other experience you have had.

  - Talk about your knowledge including—

    - American Red Cross Babysitter's Training and other certifications you have earned, such as American Red Cross First Aid and CPR—Child and Infant.

    - What you would do to be a safe and fun babysitter.

- After the interview is finished, thank the family members for their time.

Landing the Job

During the interview, parents may want to ask questions about you and your babysitting skills. Relax and be friendly. They just want to find out if you are the right babysitter for the job. If you've assessed the job and know that it's right for you, be ready to explain why you would make an excellent babysitter and you should be able to land almost any babysitting job.

Professional Behavior

The families that hire you expect you to keep their children safe, to interact with their children and to respect their homes and rules. Following the family's household rules and routines and acting in a professional manner shows families that you take your job seriously. The My Babysitting Organizer, included on the *Babysitter's Training CD-ROM,* is a tool that you can use to help keep track of all the family information you gather during the interview and as you begin babysitting for the same families again and again. Below are some professional practices you should always follow.

Before the Babysitting Job

- Treat families like customers. Show them the same respect and courtesy that you expect to be shown by them. Let them know you appreciate their business.
- Check your availability before accepting a job.
- Follow through on your word. For example, if you tell the family you will call them back the next day, be sure to do so.
- Let families know your curfew before accepting a job.
- Never babysit if you are sick.
- Only cancel a babysitting appointment for an emergency or if you are sick.
- Alert the family as far in advance as possible if you have to cancel.
- Clean your hands and fingernails.
- Dress in clean, comfortable clothes that are appropriate for babysitting. Bring an extra shirt in case of accidents.
- Only accept jobs for which you have the right skills and experience.
- Review this handbook and the emergency reference guide before each babysitting job and take them with you to each job.

During the Babysitting Job

- Arrive at the job on time or slightly early.

- Follow all of the family's instructions and household rules.

- Ask if you can use the phone. Make only necessary calls. Keep conversations brief. Never leave children alone when you are on the phone.

- If you answer a phone call, make sure to write down the message, as well as the caller's name, the time of the call and the caller's phone number.

- Ask if you and the children are allowed to use the TV, DVD, video game system, computer or any other electronic equipment. Do not use the equipment unless you have permission, even if the children have gone to bed.

- Call the parents in emergencies or for situations that you cannot handle on your own.

- Wash your hands before preparing or eating food; and after going to the bathroom, changing diapers, helping a child clean up, handling garbage, coughing or blowing your nose.

- Do not eat food unless you have been given permission.

- Clean up after eating or preparing food. Put away any toys or games that were used. Leave the house as you found it.

- Only do your homework when it is safe to do so. The children in your care come before your homework. Make sure you check your school schedule before taking babysitting assignments.

- Stay awake unless you are on an overnight job.

- Never look through rooms or belongings unless you've been asked to. Only use items for which you have permission.

- Do not have your friends come over unless you have been given permission by the family.

- Do not smoke or use drugs or alcohol.

er the Babysitting Job

- Report to the parents when they return. Note anything unusual that occurred. Use the Babysitter's Report Record found on the *Babysitter's Training CD-ROM*.
- Thank the family for their business.
- Never gossip about what you see or hear when you are babysitting. Respect the family's privacy. If you feel uncomfortable about something, discuss it with your parents.
- Keep a diary or a record of each babysitting job. Write down what went well and what did not. Note any lessons you learned or if you are interested in babysitting for this family again.
- Add notes to and update the family information in My Babysitting Organizer.
- If you want to improve your babysitting skills, then you can ask the parents for feedback about your babysitting abilities.

Remember to call your parents when you are ready to leave, unless the parents are driving you home. Do not walk home alone at night. Never accept a ride home from a babysitting job from a stranger or if you don't feel safe.

Team Resume

Directions: As a group, create a team resume. If you need help figuring out your character's background and experience or special skills and abilities, then use the assessment below.

Background and Experience

1. The number of babysitting jobs we have had is:

   ○ None   ○ 1–3   ◉ 4–6   ○ 7–10   ○ More than 10

2. The most children any of us have cared for at one time is:

   ○ 1   ○ 2   ○ 3   ◉ 4   ○ 5 or more

3. The youngest child we have ever cared for is a(n):

   ○ Infant (newborn to 12 months)

   ○ Toddler (1 to 2 years)

   ◉ Preschooler (3 to 4 years)

   ○ Younger school-age child (5, 6 and 7 years)

   ○ Older school-age child (8, 9 and 10 years)

4. The oldest child we have ever cared for is a(n):

   ○ Infant (newborn to 12 months)

   ○ Toddler (1 to 2 years)

   ○ Preschooler (3 to 4 years)

   ◉ Younger school-age child (5, 6 and 7 years)

   ○ Older school-age child (8, 9 and 10 years)

5. Our longest babysitting job lasted:

   ○ 1 hour   ○ 2–3 hours   ◉ 3–5 hours   ○ 5–8 hours

   ○ More than 8 hours

6. We have worked babysitting jobs (check all that apply):

- ⭕ On weekdays
- 🔘 In my neighborhood
- ⭕ On weeknights
- ⭕ Outside my neighborhood
- ⭕ On weekend days
- ⭕ During vacation times
- ⭕ On weekend nights
- ⭕ During the school year

Special Skills and Abilities

7. Our special abilities include (check all that apply):

- ⭕ Music
- ⊗ Patience
- ⊗ Arts and crafts
- ⊗ Creativity
- ⊗ Sports
- ⊗ Good student
- ⭕ Storytelling
- ⭕ Sense of humor
- ⭕ Other: _____

8. Our babysitting skills include (rate your ability):

Making good decisions

| Very good ⭕ | Good 🔘 | Needs work ⭕ |

Problem solving

| Very good ⭕ | Good 🔘 | Needs work ⭕ |

Staying calm in an emergency

| Very good ⭕ | Good ⭕ | Needs work 🔘 |

Communicating well with children

| Very good 🔘 | Good ⭕ | Needs work ⭕ |

Role modeling positive behavior

| Very good ⭕ | Good 🔘 | Needs work ⭕ |

Recognizing and respecting differences among children and families

| Very good 🔘 | Good ⭕ | Needs work ⭕ |

Correcting misbehavior appropriately

| Very good 🔘 | Good ⭕ | Needs work ⭕ |

Recognizing and making considerations for the developmental stages of children at different ages

Very good ◯   Good ◉   Needs work ◯

Assessing babysitting jobs and gathering the necessary information before they begin

Very good ◯   Good ◉   Needs work ◯

Acting professionally at all times

Very good ◯   Good ◉   Needs work ◯

Diapering

Very good ◯   Good ◉   Needs work ◯

Feeding children with a bottle or a spoon

Very good ◉   Good ◯   Needs work ◯

Helping children get rest and sleep

Very good ◉   Good ◯   Needs work ◯

Picking up and holding children correctly

Very good ◉   Good ◯   Needs work ◯

Giving appropriate care for children of different ages

Very good ◉   Good ◯   Needs work ◯

Check all that apply:

◯ Being certified in American Red Cross CPR—Child and Infant

◯ Being certified in American Red Cross Standard First Aid

Team Job Interview

Directions: Using the information on pages 19-20 in your handbook, write down five questions you should ask during the family interview.

_____
_____
_____
_____
_____
_____
_____

Using your group resume and the tips on how to ace an interview on page 21 in your handbook, write down five things you can do during a babysitting job interview that will help you land the job.

_____
_____
_____
_____
_____
_____
_____

Your classroom instructor will be asking you some "what if" questions about how you might act in certain situations. Using the information on professional behavior on pages 22-24 in your handbook to help you prepare, be ready to answer the following questions:

What would you do if you started feeling sick one hour before your babysitting job begins?

_____
_____
_____
_____
_____
_____

What would you do if the family asked you to help their children with homework on a subject that you did not know or understand?

_____
_____
_____
_____
_____
_____

What would you do if you found out you had to study for a really big test on the same night as your babysitting job?

_____
_____
_____
_____
_____
_____

What would you do if the children asked if you would bake them some cookies, but the parents told you not to use the oven?

_____
_____
_____
_____
_____
_____

What would you do if you broke a plate while cleaning up after a snack?

_____

_____

_____

_____

_____

What would you do if one of the parents received an important call? For example, a grandparent has been hospitalized.

_____

_____

_____

_____

_____

What would you do if the family was late returning home and had not called you yet?

_____

_____

_____

_____

_____

CHAPTER 3

Safe and Sound on the Job

As a babysitter, your most important responsibility is to keep children safe while their parents are away.

In this chapter, you will find many helpful lists that highlight what you need to do to keep yourself and the children you are watching safe. This chapter will also teach you how to avoid injuries and illnesses by following guidelines on how to prevent, recognize and, if needed, fix safety-related problems. Use the lists in this chapter to guide you in keeping the house and the children you watch safe.

Telephone Safety Tips

It is hard to supervise children while you're talking on the telephone. That's why you should keep all conversations as short as possible and avoid personal calls that aren't absolutely necessary. You should also not use your mobile phone to text message or talk unnecessarily. Here are some things to keep in mind about telephone use when you are babysitting:

- Ask the parents if and how they would like their phone answered.
- Be polite and brief when answering the phone.
- Use the phone for calls related to the job only, not for personal calls, unless the parents have given you permission to use it for a short personal call (e.g., you need a homework question answered from a friend).
- Remember that you may tie up the phone line when you use the Internet; so keep your time on the Internet brief.
- Keep all conversations as short as possible and avoid personal calls that aren't absolutely necessary.
- Call the parents, an adult you trust or the police if you get a call that scares you.
- Make sure emergency phone numbers, the address of where you are babysitting, a pen/pencil and paper are posted by all phones.
- NEVER leave the children alone while answering the phone.
- Do not tell the caller that you are the babysitter or that the parents are away. Instead, say, "Mr. or Mrs. _____ is busy right now. May I take a message?"
- Do not call, text message or instant message your friends or have them call you for a long conversation while on the job. Even if you are using your personal mobile phone, you could miss an important call from the children's parents or you may not know if the children call for you or become ill. Also, the children could end up in an unsafe situation and possibly get hurt if you are not supervising them closely.

Personal Safety

Your own health and safety are just as important as the health and safety of the children you babysit. Here are some ways to keep yourself healthy and safe while babysitting:

- Get to know the parents and families of the children you babysit and meet their pets.
- Tell your parents where you will be, when to expect you home and how to contact you. Know where they will be and how to contact them (see "Getting Started" on page 14 for more information).
- If babysitting for a certain family makes you feel uncomfortable, don't babysit for them.
- If you get to a babysitting job and you feel you are in danger or your personal safety may be at risk, don't be afraid to say no to the job.
- Make your own arrangements to get to and from the job safely. Have a back-up plan ready. For example, if you are uncomfortable riding home with the child's parent, have a code word that you can use on the telephone to let your parents know that you need a ride home from them. A code word could be, "How is *Otis* doing?" Or saying, "I am glad it's *summertime*."
- Do not wear jewelry that dangles or has sharp edges. It can scratch or hurt you or the children.
- Keep your clothing out of the way and your hair neat so they don't get caught in anything.
- Keep your fingernails short and your hands clean to prevent the spread of germs.
- Do not babysit when you are sick.
- Do not use alcohol, tobacco or other drugs.
- Keep your first aid kit handy but out of the children's reach.
- Know what you can and cannot do and respect those limits.
- Take your *Babysitter's Training Handbook* and *Emergency Reference Guide* with you and use it as a reference while on the job.

Danger from Strangers

- When in the home, never open the door to strangers. Always check before opening the door to anyone, even the parents. Look out through a peephole or window first.

- Never open the door to delivery people or service representatives. Ask delivery people to leave the package at the door or tell them to come back another time. Service representatives, such as a cable installer or an electrician, should have an appointment when the parents are home.

- Do not go outside to check out an unusual noise. If you are worried about it, call the parents, an adult you trust or the police.

- If you leave the home, such as if you go to the park, do not talk to strangers. If a stranger keeps trying to talk to you, ignore the person and take the children to a safe area.

- If you are visiting a public place, such as a park, check that restrooms are clean and safe for children before allowing them to use the restroom. Do not leave children alone when you inspect or use a restroom and do not allow children to go into the restroom by themselves. Make sure to check the restroom for people and if anyone looks suspicious, leave the restroom.

Other Safety Considerations
Inside the Home

- If the family has a home electronic security system, ask the parents if they would like you to use it, and have them demonstrate how to turn it on and off.

- Do not have your friends over to visit while you are babysitting unless previously discussed with the parents and noted on the Family Interview Form, found on the *Babysitter's Training CD-ROM*.

- Do not let anyone inside who is using alcohol or drugs, even if it is someone you know.

- Do not stay in a situation where you or the children are being threatened by a parent, guardian or anyone else. Immediately take the children to a safe place such as a neighbor's home; a school; a church, mosque or synagogue; a local business; or a police or fire station.

- Do not stay anywhere that you smell smoke or hear a fire or smoke alarm. Get the children and yourself outside. Ask a neighbor to call the fire department.

Outside the Home

- Be aware of the sun and take precautions to protect yourself and the children against damage from the sun.

- Lock the door when you leave the house and make sure all the windows are closed and locked.

- Never leave the house without the parent's permission. If you and the children do leave, tell someone where you are going, when you will leave and when you will be back, then call when you return. Never leave the house without the children even for a short period of time (e.g., to bring a pet back into the house or to get a toy from the driveway).

Safety Inspection Checklist

Take a copy of the Safety Inspection Checklist with you each time you babysit. Use it to help you recognize and prevent safety-related problems that you may run into on the job. Additonal copies of the Safety Inspection Checklist can be printed from the *Babysitter's Training CD-ROM.*

RURAL SAFETY

If your babysitting job is in a rural area, you will need to be aware of some additional safety hazards. During the family interview, ask where the children are allowed to be and which areas are not safe for them. Be sure to get a detailed explanation. Ask if there are buildings, such as barns or storage areas, that are off-limits to the children. Likewise, find out if there are off-limit outside areas, such as ponds or fields where animals are kept.

It's also a good idea to ask the parents to take you on a walk around the property to note the possible hazards. These can include—

- Water, such as ponds or lakes.
- Farm equipment and machinery.
- Farm animals.
- Electric fences.

Some children, especially those who live on farms, may have chores they need to complete while you are babysitting them. Make sure to ask the parents what the children are allowed to do and supervise children at all times.

In rural areas, remember that response time for emergency medical services (EMS) personnel is longer and that the nearest neighbor may be far away.

Safety **INSPECTION** **CHECKLIST**—Check It Out!

For Emergencies

○ The emergency phone list has been filled out and is posted.

○ The first aid kit is properly stocked and stored away.

○ I know where the working flashlights, battery-operated radio and extra batteries are located.

To Prevent Wounds

○ Knives, hand tools, power tools, razor blades, scissors, guns, ammunition and other objects that can cause injury are stored in locked cabinets or locked storage areas.

To Prevent Falls

○ Safety gates are installed at all open stairways in homes with small children and infants.

○ Windows and balcony doors have childproof latches or window guards.

○ Balconies have protective barriers to prevent children from slipping through the bars.

○ The home is free of clutter on the floors, especially on or near stairways.

To Prevent Poisoning

○ Potential poisons, like detergents, polishes, pesticides, car-care fluids, lighter fluids and lamp oils, are stored in locked cabinets and are out of the reach of children.

○ Houseplants are kept out of reach.

○ Medicine is kept in a locked storage place that children can't reach.

○ Child-resistant packaging is closed or reclosed securely.

To Prevent Burns

- ○ Safety covers are placed on all unused electrical outlets.
- ○ Loose cords are secured and out of the way. Multi-cord or octopus plugs are not used.
- ○ At least one approved smoke alarm is installed and operating on each level of the home.
- ○ Space heaters are placed out of the reach of children and away from curtains.
- ○ Flammable liquids are securely stored in their original containers and away from heat.
- ○ Matches and lighters are stored out of the reach of children.
- ○ Garbage and recycling materials are stored in covered containers.

To Prevent Drowning

- ○ Swimming pools and hot tubs are completely enclosed with a barrier, such as a locked fence or gate, and covered.
- ○ Wading pools and bathtubs are emptied when not in use.
- ○ Toilet seats and lids are kept down when not in use.
- ○ Bathroom doors are kept closed at all times.
- ○ Buckets or other containers with standing water are securely covered or emptied of water.

To Prevent Choking and Other Breathing Dangers

- ○ Small objects are kept out of children's reach.
- ○ Toy box has ventilation holes. If there is a lid, it is lightweight and removable and has a sliding door or panel or is a hinged lid with a support to hold it open.
- ○ The crib mattress fits the side of the crib snugly and toys, blankets and pillows are removed from the crib.
- ○ Drape and blind cords are wound up and not dangling.

Hazard Hunt

Directions: *As you watch the video segment, "Hazard Hunt," write a one- or two-word description of each safety-related problem you find in the video.*

Safety-Related Problem

Entry Hall
Skate bord and toys no
Baby gate

Living Room
toys, Lamb, TV, Fire Things

Kitchen
glass, Hot Pot, Sissors
Knife, Step Stool, Food

Bathroom
Clearss, open Sheifs with
medcines, toys Hair dryer

Bedroom
toys in crib, drawers open
money, Lamp

Utility Room
Soap, cleaers open dryer

Playroom
toys, cords, popcorn

Backyard
Wood every where, fire pit
hose, Ladder

Preventing Accidents and Injuries

Accidental injuries are the leading cause of death of children over the age of 1. Fortunately, most accidental injuries can be prevented. As a babysitter it is important that you learn to prevent, recognize and fix safety-related problems.

A babysitter's first priority is to prevent accidents from happening in the first place by making sure that the home and the activities the children participate in are safe. The best way to do this is to use the Family Interview Form as you talk to the children's parents, and then walk through the home as you complete the Safety Inspection Checklist. However, there will always be situations in which there will be little you can do to **prevent** a safety-related problem from occurring in the first place; therefore, when you are babysitting you will always need to be on the lookout for safety-related problems so you can **recognize** them before an accident or injury occurs and take quick action to **fix** them once noticed.

Below you will find 11 safety-related problems that you might encounter while babysitting. Each problem is followed by three lists. The first gives you tips for preventing the problem in the first place, the second includes ways to recognize that the problem exists and the third tells you how to fix specific sample problems once you have noticed them.

Bites and Stings
Prevent the Safety-Related Problem

- Know what animals and insects are common to your area and how to avoid them.

- Stay away from any wild animal or pet that you recognize as acting strangely.

- Use appropriate insect repellant that has been approved by the parents to help keep biting insects away.

- Have children wear shoes and socks and keep arms and legs covered with long-sleeve shirts and long pants if playing in or near wooded areas.
- Find out in advance if the children have allergic reactions to insect bites or stings. If so, find out what to do if these occur.

Recognize the Safety-Related Problem

- Be on the lookout for insects and other animals that may bite, sting or otherwise hurt the children.
- If a child is bitten or stung by an insect, watch for any signals of an allergic reaction.

Fix the Safety-Related Problem

- If children start to dig or reach into areas where animals or insects may live, such as in woodpiles, near garbage, under logs or in leaves or brush, stop them!
- If you come upon an area with insects that may bite or sting, leave the area.
- If an animal appears to be rabid or unfriendly, leave the area.

Burns
Prevent the Safety-Related Problem

- Keep children and pets at least 3 feet away from any heat source, such as hot food or liquid, table lamps and a stove or oven that is in use. Do not leave items in or on the stove unattended.
- Turn pot handles toward the back of the stove, out of the reach of children, when cooking.
- Use back/rear burners for cooking whenever possible.
- Tuck away loose clothing and roll up sleeves when using the stove.
- NEVER hold a child and cook at the same time.
- Always use hot pads or oven mitts to remove pots and pans from the stove or oven and keep them close when cooking. Never use a wet oven mitt.
- Always place hot items, including hot liquids, out of the reach of children.
- Stir any food that has been warmed in the microwave and make sure to test the temperature.
- Be sure that warmed bottles and food are not too hot by testing the temperature before feeding them to children and infants. NEVER use a microwave to warm a bottle; hot spots could potentially burn them.
- Do not let children climb on stoves or cooking surfaces.

- Make sure all unused electrical outlets have safety covers and do not let children play with the safety covers.
- Keep appliance cords out of the reach of children.
- Make sure you and the children use sunscreen for outdoor activities, stay out of direct sunlight during prime sun hours (10 a.m.–4 p.m.) and wear protective clothing, such as a hat, long-sleeved shirt, pants and sunglasses.
- Be sure that bath water is not too hot by testing the temperature with your elbow before bathing children.

Recognize the Safety-Related Problem

- Be on the lookout for anything hot that could burn children, including food, water, table lamps, heaters, stoves or ovens and even the sun.

KITCHEN FIRES

Even a small kitchen fire can spread quickly. If you are in doubt, get yourself and the children out of the house and then call the fire department. Keep these tips in mind for preventing and, if possible, containing kitchen fires.

- If a small fire starts in a pan on the stove, put on an oven mitt and smother the flames by carefully sliding the lid over the pan. Turn off the burner. Leave the lid on the pan until the pan is completely cool. Never pour water on and never discharge a fire extinguisher onto a grease fire, as it can spray or shoot burning grease around the kitchen, causing the fire to spread.
- If there is a fire in the oven, turn off the heat and keep the door closed.
- Never use aluminum foil or metal objects in a microwave. They can cause a fire or burn hazard and damage the microwave.
- If you have a fire in your microwave, turn it off immediately, if you can safely reach the outlet, unplug it and keep the door closed. Leave the door closed until the fire is completely out. If you are in doubt, get out and call the fire department.
- Remember your responsibility as a babysitter during any fire is to get the kids safely out of the house and call the fire department.

Fix the Safety-Related Problem

- If a child approaches you as you are cooking on the stove, then stop and ask the child to stay back. Put him or her at a safe distance (at least 3 feet) until you are finished cooking.

- If you see a that a child's attention is captured by an electrical outlet and you think he or she might insert something into it, make him or her stop. Distract the child's attention so that he or she becomes interested in a different activity.

Choking and Breathing Dangers

Choking is an emergency in which children or infants cannot cough, speak, cry or breathe because the airway is partially or completely blocked.

Prevent the Safety-Related Problem

- Always have children sit up when eating.
- Feed infants and toddlers soft food in small and age-appropriate amounts that are easy to chew.
- Do not let children walk, run, play or talk with food or other objects in their mouths.
- Cut food into small pieces.
- Encourage children to take small bites and chew thoroughly.
- Do not feed infants and toddlers foods that pose choking dangers including—
  - Small food like raisins, popcorn, nuts, hard candy, grapes, chips, hot dog slices, raw vegetables and marshmallows.
  - Large food items that break into small pieces like teething biscuits and cookies.
  - Sticky food like peanut butter.
- Make sure children play with toys that are safe and appropriate for their age.
- Keep play areas clear of small objects and clean up after playing.
- Do not dress children in clothing with drawstrings longer than 3 inches. Sleepwear should not have any drawstrings.
- Keep drape and blind cords wound up so they are not dangling.

Recognize the Safety-Related Problem

- Look around the home and play areas for small objects that could cause choking.
- Watch for unsafe eating habits, such as talking or running while eating.

Note: Be aware and especially careful with infants and toddlers. Many infants and toddlers explore by putting things in their mouths and can easily choke on them.

Fix the Safety-Related Problem

- If objects that could choke or suffocate a young child are out and accessible, put or take them away. Examples include plastic bags; balloons; small balls, marbles and toys intended for older children; disposable gloves; beads; pebbles; buttons; caps; hairpins; coins; jewelry; and toys with long strings.
- If a young child is going to play with stuffed animals, dolls or action figures, check to make sure eyes, noses, buttons and other small parts are securely attached.
- If there is anything in a child's or infant's crib, take it out. Before putting the baby down to sleep, remove from the crib all small objects, soft bedding and other smothering risks such as pillows, blankets, cushions and beanbags that can wrap around or cover the face of a small child or infant. The U.S. Consumer Product Safety Commission, the American Academy of Pediatrics and the National Institute of Child Health and Human Development Back to Sleep Campaign recommend the following: "If using a blanket, put the baby with his or her feet at the foot of the crib. Tuck a thin blanket around the crib mattress, reaching only to the baby's chest." (see "Sudden Infant Death Syndrome," page 92).
- If a child is walking around the house with food in his or her mouth, tell the child to stop and sit down at the table while he or she is eating.

Drowning

A drowning can occur when a child's face is submerged in any depth of water for too long and can happen in a bathtub, bucket or even a toilet bowl.

Prevent the Safety-Related Problem

- NEVER leave children alone, even for a moment, in a bathtub or near any water, even a bucket with a small amount of water. Always stay within arm's reach of a child near water.
- Keep bathroom doors closed and toilet lids down.

- Bathe children only if you have been taught how to do so, feel comfortable doing so and have the parents' approval. If you are watching more than one young child, do not give a bath to one of the children if you cannot properly supervise all children.

- For a home with a swimming pool, be sure that all gates and doors leading to the pool area are locked. Also, keep pool toys out of the water and put them away out of the children's sight.

- If you take the children swimming to a public facility, be sure trained lifeguards are on duty. Even when lifeguards are present, you are still responsible for supervising the children in your care.

- NEVER trust inflatable flotation devices or bath seats to prevent drowning. Always stay within arm's reach of the child and use a Coast Guard-approved personal flotation device (PFD). Check for a Coast Guard-approved label on the PFD.

- For a home with a hot tub, be sure that it is covered and secured.

Recognize the Safety-Related Problem

- Understand that younger children can drown at any moment, even in an inch of water.

- Look for sources of water in and around the home where children could potentially drown.

- Check to see if there are trained lifeguards on duty whenever going swimming at a public facility.

- For homes with a pool, check to see that all gates and doors that lead to the pool area are locked.

- Only take the children swimming if you can swim and are comfortable in and around the water. If you are interested in learning to swim, then find out about American Red Cross swim lessons. If you want more information on the basics of water safety, sign up for Red Cross Basic Water Rescue or GuardStart: Lifeguarding Tomorrow.

Fix the Safety-Related Problem

- If there is standing water anywhere, such as in a wading pool, bathtub or bucket, empty it of all water.

- If the home has a swimming pool, keep children away from the pool area, unless it is designated swim time and you are within arm's reach of the children at all times. Even if gates are secure, never leave a child near the pool area alone.

Falls
Prevent the Safety-Related Problem

- Have children wear helmets and protective padding, such as knee or elbow guards when using riding toys.
- Do not dress children in loose-fitting clothes or clothes that are too big; these can be a tripping hazard.
- Make sure shoes are not too big and that laces are snuggly tied.
- Do not allow children to climb on furniture.
- Keep infants and small children away from stairs.
- Remove extra toys from play areas.
- Keep doors and traffic paths clear of electrical cords and other items.
- Push chairs in under tables and desks.
- Put away stools and ladders.
- Keep beds, end tables and other furniture away from windows.
- Keep windows and doors locked.

Recognize the Safety-Related Problem

- Look for anything that could cause anyone—infants, children or even you—to trip or fall.

Fix the Safety-Related Problem

- If toys, books, shoes or other items are on the stairs, remove the clutter.
- If electrical cords, furniture or toys are in traffic paths that could cause someone to trip or fall, clear the space.
- If gates and doors leading to stairs are open, close them.

Fire (Heat Sources)
Prevent the Safety-Related Problem

- Talk to parents about a Family Fire Escape Plan that shows at least two exits out of every room. Families can find out more about how to be prepared for fires and other emergencies by contacting their local American Red Cross chapter or by visiting *www.redcross.org/disaster/masters*.
- Learn when and how to use a fire extinguisher and where it is kept. Ask your local fire department for more information and about getting trained.
- Make sure children know how to Stop, Drop and Roll if clothing catches on fire.

- Make sure children know how to crawl low under smoke and test for hot doors before opening them during a fire escape.

- Know where fire stairs, fire exits and escape ladders are located in high-rise buildings and how to use them.

- Know where fire alarms and smoke alarms are located.

- Do not leave items in or on the stove unattended.

- Keep matches and lighters out of the reach of children.

- Do not light candles, incense, scented candles, oil lamps or lights.

- Keep electrical equipment away from water; they can create sparks if contact with water is made.

Recognize the Safety-Related Problem

- Be careful around any source of heat, such as stoves, heaters, fireplaces and grills.

Fix the Safety-Related Problem

- If using any heat source, clear the space of toys, curtains and similar items. These items should be at least 3 feet away from the heat source.

- If using space heaters, turn them off before you go to sleep or leave the area. Do not use space heaters unless instructed to do so by the parents.

If a Fire Occurs

Your first priority is to get yourself and the children out of the area. Get out and stay out! Your job is to protect the children and yourself, not household belongings. Once you are away from the fire, find the nearest adult or call 9-1-1 or the local emergency number right away! NEVER return to a burning building.

Illnesses
Prevent the Safety-Related Problem

- Keep toys clean.

- Use tissues and cover your mouth and nose when coughing and sneezing. If you don't have a tissue, cough or sneeze into the inside of your elbow or upper arm.

- Keep trash out of the reach of children.
- Refrigerate foods that can spoil.
- If you or the children touch any animal or its droppings, wash hands with warm water and soap.
- Teach and practice good health habits, such as washing hands.
- Have children and infants wash their hands before and after eating and after toileting or diapering, coughing, sneezing or blowing their noses.
- Eat healthy, get plenty of rest and exercise regularly. All of these things help your body fight infection.

Recognize the Safety-Related Problem

- Although germs are present in most places, you can keep them from entering the body and causing illness.
- Watch for signs that you, the children or others around you are feeling ill.

Fix the Safety-Related Problem

- If you feel sick or are ill, do not babysit.
- If you use the restroom, change diapers, cough, sneeze or blow your nose, wash your hands. Also, always be sure to wash your hands before and after preparing food and after giving first aid.

Poisoning
Prevent the Safety-Related Problem

- Only use nontoxic markers, glue and other art supplies.
- Only give a child or an infant medicine when directed by the parent to do so. Ask the parents to provide clearly written instructions on how to give the medication to the child or infant and the correct dosage. They should provide this information on the Parental Consent and Contact Form.
- Always read the label; make sure it is the right medication and dosage.
- Record what medicine you gave and the time you gave it on the Babysitter's Report Record.
- Never transfer products and medicines out of child-resistant containers. Do not mix infant medicine in with a bottle as the infant may not finish the bottle.
- Keep all poisonous substances out of the reach of children or in cabinets and drawers with safety latches or locks. Some common poisonous substances inside and around the home include alcohol, drugs,

medicines, vitamins, lighter fluid, lamp oil, hair and beauty products, baby oil, tobacco, cleaning products, paints, bug and weed killers and car products.

○ When using cleaning products, follow the BEFORE, WHILE and AFTER rule:

  ○ BEFORE using a cleaning product, read the instructions.

  ○ WHILE using a cleaning product, never leave it alone. Children may find it.

  ○ AFTER using a cleaning product, put it back in a locked cabinet immediately. Make sure the container is closed tightly.

○ Keep children away from plants that they could put into their mouths.

○ Do not let children play near peeling paint or plaster.

Recognize the Safety-Related Problem

○ Know what items can be poisonous to children and infants.

○ Be on the lookout for poisonous substances inside and around the home.

Fix the Safety-Related Problem

○ If parents ask you to give children medicine, make them aware that they are getting medicine. Don't call it "candy."

○ If you think you might touch any chemicals or poisons, use disposable gloves.

○ If there are any cabinets or doors without locks that may contain poisons, keep children away from the area.

Riding Toy/Vehicle Injuries
Prevent the Safety-Related Problem

○ Have children wear appropriate helmets and protective padding, such as knee or elbow guards, when using bicycles, skate boards and other riding toys.

○ Have children use caution and sit where they should when driving a battery-powered riding toy or other vehicle.

○ Dress children in bright colors so that they can easily be seen.

○ Dress children in clothes that fit well and do not have anything hanging or loose and make sure shoe laces are snugly tied. Otherwise, their clothing could get caught in wheels or other moving parts.

○ Keep children away from curbs, parked cars, hilly areas and streets.

- Teach safety rules for crossing the street, including—
  - Holding hands when crossing the street.
  - Looking both ways before crossing.
  - Crossing only at the crosswalk.
  - Not crossing the street without a grown-up or a responsible person, such as a babysitter.

Recognize the Safety-Related Problem

- Know that accidents with riding toys and motor vehicles can cause serious injuries.

Fix the Safety-Related Problem

- If the children are playing on riding toys, make sure their clothes fit appropriately with nothing loose or hanging and that their shoe laces are snugly tied.
- If the children start driving their riding toys near pools, on hilly or steep ground, in streets or on steps, ask them to stop immediately and direct them to a safe place to ride.

Parks and Outdoors
Prevent the Safety-Related Problem

- Keep children away from curbs, parked cars, hilly areas and streets.
- Check the nearby area for rough spots, holes and any objects that could trip children.
- Watch out for poisonous plants; plants with thorns, stickers and roots that stick up; and trees with low branches that could cause scratches.
- Check for trash; broken glass or cement; needles; animal droppings; sewage; and shiny objects, like open aluminum cans, which may be sharp and can cause wounds.
- Check that restrooms are clean and safe for children; do not leave the children alone when you inspect a restroom. Make sure to check the restroom for people. If anyone looks suspicious, leave the restroom. Do not allow children to go into restrooms by themselves.
- Inspect play equipment and make sure it is in good condition. Look for openings or railings that could trap a child's hands, head or feet. Any space larger than the width of a soda can is unsafe. Supervise children at all times on the play equipment.

- Don't dress children in clothes that could catch on playground equipment, such as clothes with drawstrings and hoods.
- Make sure children's clothing is appropriate for the activity and make adjustments when needed. For example, tuck pants into socks to protect yourself and the children from tick bites and other insects when playing around wooded, brushy or tall grassy areas.
- Check for sand, wood chips or rubber matting under play equipment to cushion children's falls.
- Check that the sand in sandboxes is clean and safe.
- Watch out for loose animals.
- Watch out for storm drains and keep the children away from them, especially after a rainstorm.
- Check for any water in the area, such as a fountain, pond or a lake. Do not allow the children to play near the water unless you are within arm's reach of them.
- Use appropriate insect repellant that has been approved by the parents to help keep biting or stinging insects away.
- Teach safety rules for crossing the street, including—
  - Holding hands when crossing the street.
  - Looking both ways before crossing.
  - Crossing only at the crosswalk.
  - Crossing the street only with a grown-up or a responsible person, such as a babysitter.

Recognize the Safety-Related Problem

- Outdoor environments present special hazards and dangers to children, which can cause serious injuries or illnesses. Always be on the lookout for potential dangers while playing outside.
- Make sure that the children stay close by so you can see and hear them.

Fix the Safety-Related Problem

- If you see any sharp objects, such as broken glass or rusty nails, throw them away.
- If you see poisonous plants, water and other hazards, move away from the area.
- If you have been playing outside in a wooded, brushy or tall grassy area, check children and their clothing for ticks and other insects before entering the house.

SAFE FUN IN THE SUN

In addition to painful sunburn, overexposure from the sun's harmful ultraviolet (UV) rays can cause skin cancer, eye damage and premature aging. It can also suppress your immune system, which makes it harder for your body to fight off disease.

The risk of getting skin cancer is higher for those who burn easily or have a history of bad sunburns. People with the following features are also at higher risk:

- Blond or red hair
- Blue, green, gray or hazel eyes
- Fair skin and easily freckled
- Many moles
- Family history of cancer

Luckily, you can have fun in the sun, while protecting yourself and the children from harmful UV rays. To keep everyone safe, follow the tips below.

- Notice the time of day before going outside. UV rays are strongest between 10 a.m. and 4 p.m. During these hours, avoid exposure to the sun or seek shade, if possible.
- Always use sunscreen, even on a cloudy day. You can still burn when it's cloudy. You can also burn when near windows, at home or in a car.
- Apply sunscreen 20 minutes before you go outside. Reapply every 2 hours and after swimming or sweating.
- Make sure your sunscreen has a sun protection factor (SPF) of at least 15 and preferably 30 or higher. Remember to check with parents before putting sunscreen on children to make sure they don't have any allergies or sensitivities.
- Apply sunscreen to infants if approved by the parents. Only use sunscreen that is recommended for use on infants. When putting sunscreen on infants under 6 months old, apply a small amount on the face and the back of the hands, if adequate clothing and shade are not available and the parents have asked you to do so.
- Wear protective clothing, like long-sleeved shirts, long pants, a hat and sunglasses, whenever possible.
- Don't lay out in the sun to tan.
- Be careful around water, snow and sand. Your exposure to UV rays increases because the rays reflect off these surfaces.
- Check out the UV index. This daily forecast of UV levels can help you plan outdoor activities for safe times of the day. (To view the UV index, go to: *www.epa.gov/sunwise/uvindex.html*)

If an emergency does happen…

Make sure you have coins or a mobile phone for an emergency telephone call to the parents. You do not need to pay to call 9-1-1 from a pay phone. If you use a mobile phone, make sure you understand how to use it and that the battery is charged. Remember to bring the parents' contact numbers with you when are outside of the home. You also need to know exactly where you are, such as the name of the park and the nearest street, so you can let the parents or emergency personnel know, if necessary.

Wounds

Prevent the Safety-Related Problem

- Keep all running or jumping games and activities away from large glass doors or windows.
- Keep play areas free of sharp objects.
- Make sure all sharp and dangerous objects, such as knives, saws, hammers, screwdrivers, power tools, guns and ammunition, are out of the reach of children.
- Make sure children always wear shoes when playing outside.
- Use proper protective gear for outdoor activities, such as helmets, knee pads and elbow pads for bike riding and skate boarding.
- Closely supervise all play.

Recognize the Safety-Related Problem

- Look for toys with sharp edges.
- Check rooms and outside play areas for objects or surfaces that could harm children, including glass and other sharp objects.

Fix the Safety-Related Problem

- If you see any sharp objects, remove them so they are out of the children's reach.
- If children's play becomes rough, especially near large glass doors or windows, change the activity to something calmer to settle them down.

Being Prepared for Weather Emergencies

It is very important for babysitters to know how to prevent, prepare for and respond to weather-related emergencies.

Before every babysitting job, check your Family Interview Form, found on the *Babysitter's Training CD-ROM*, to see what instructions the parents have given to follow in case of an emergency. If you find yourself faced with a possible or actual weather emergency, then take the following steps:

Electrical Storms (Thunderstorms)

- If you are outside, go inside a safe structure such as a house or building to seek shelter. DO NOT go under a tree, shed or other yard structure.
- Stay off the telephone during storms.
- Don't shower, bathe or touch water.
- Know where working flashlights and extra batteries are kept.
- If the power goes out, use alternative lighting, such as lightsticks or flashlights. Never use candles.
- Turn off and unplug electrical appliances, such as the TV or computer.
- Keep children near you during storms and power outages and comfort and reassure them.

Floods, Earthquakes, Tornadoes, Winter Storms and Hurricanes

- Listen to local radio or TV stations for instructions on what to do and where to go.
- In case of tornadoes or high winds, keep children away from windows and take them to the basement or an inner room if there is no basement.
- Know where to take the children for shelter, especially if you are in a mobile home.
- Know where to take cover if you feel the ground shaking.
- Know where and how to turn off the utilities.
- During winter storms, keep children inside and warm.
- Know the family plan in case of storms or other disasters.
- Know where the disaster supplies kit is kept and what's in it; it should be well stocked.
- If you have to take the children to a shelter, let the parents know where you are going, if possible, and try to contact them when you get there.

Go to the American Red Cross Disaster Services Web site at *www.redcross.org/images/pdfs/code/disaster_supplies_kit.pdf* for a list of disaster supplies kit contents. For information on a variety of training opportunities, including disaster preparedness, home safety and personal safety, contact your local Red Cross chapter.

Violence or Crime

- Be aware of your surroundings and what is going on around you.
- Avoid drawing unwanted attention to yourself when you are away from the house. Dangerous people may cause you or the children harm simply because of what you are wearing or because of something you say.
- Know how to open security bars or doors, where emergency exits are located and how to get out of the house or apartment building.
- If you hear gunfire, you and the children should lie down on the ground or floor, cover your head with your hands and wait for 20 to 30 minutes before leaving cover. Call 9-1-1 or the local emergency number as soon as you possibly can.
- If it looks as if the home has been broken into when you return from an outing, DO NOT enter. Take the children to a safe place, such as a designated neighbor or a local business, and call 9-1-1 or the local emergency number. You can even go to a police or fire station. Remember to contact the parents right away after getting help. Your job is to protect yourself and the children, not household belongings.

Play It Safe!

Keep children safe during play by watching them at all times. While you play with the children, watch how they act, learn what activities they like best and discover how they want to play.

- Follow the family's rules for play. (See the Family Interview Form found on the *Babysitter's Training CD-ROM*.)
- Choose the right toys and games for each child, based on his or her age and likes and dislikes. Safety depends on the right toy and activity at the right age.

- Actively play with the children—don't just watch them.

- Remember to read all directions and warnings on children's toys and games to find out the recommended ages and how to use them properly.

Choose the toys and activities that are safe and right for each child. The following table will give you some suggestions for safe toys and activities based on children's ages.

NOTE: *For infants and toddlers, in general, no toy should be smaller than 1¾ inches in diameter (Fig. 3-1). Most toys are labeled and will clearly say if the toy is safe for the age group.*

FIGURE 3-1

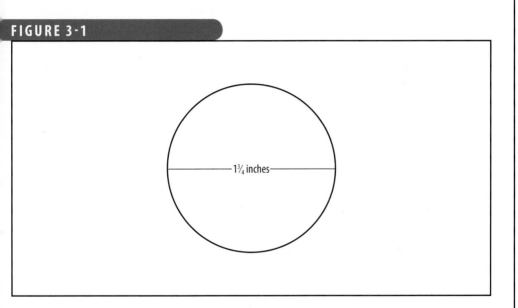

Safety and Toys

Infants (Newborn to 6 Months)	Infants (6 Months to 12 Months)	Toddlers (1 and 2 Year Olds)
• Soft mobiles • Rattles • Soft fabric swatches • Stuffed animals	• Large colored blocks made of rubber or soft material • Large stacking boxes or cups • Squeaky toys or bells • Large balls • Pots and pans • Wooden spoons and plastic bowls • Simple picture books or cloth books • Push-pull toys • Teething toys	• Building blocks • Large plastic toy people and animals • Action toys like telephones, trains, planes, cars and trucks • Simple puzzles with knobs • Puppets • Large balls • Staple-free cardboard boxes • Books • Drums, xylophone and other musical toys • Pail and shovel • Riding toys

For a free copy of the publication, "Which Toy for Which Child: Ages Birth through 5," write for item #285 and for "Which Toy for Which Child: Ages 6-12," write for item #286, U.S. Consumer Product Safety Commission, Washington, DC 20207. More safety information is available at *www.cpsc.gov* or by calling the Consumer Product Safety Commission's toll-free hotline at (800) 638-2772.

Safety and Toys—cont'd

Preschoolers (3 and 4 Year Olds)	Younger School-Age Children (5, 6 and 7 Year Olds)	Older School-Age Children (8, 9 and 10 Year Olds)
• Playground equipment like see-saws, swings, slides and climbing structures (if closely supervised) • Simple board games • Storybooks • Balls • Musical instruments • Dolls, action figures and props for pretend play—cooking, cleaning and carpentry • Wagons and tricycles • Puzzles with large pieces • Sandbox and water table (if closely supervised) • Electronic games	• Board games and puzzles • Items related to hobbies or collections like stickers, rocks or miniature cars • Electronic games • Fashion and action dolls • Bikes and scooters	• Sports equipment • Bikes • Remote control cars • Construction sets

CHAPTER 4

Understanding Kids from 0 to 10

Everyone has a job to do.

Adults have to work and take care of their families. Older children have homework and chores. Some older children take on important jobs like babysitting! The main job of young children is to play; it is a very important part of their growth and development. One of the main duties of a babysitter is to guide children in safe, fun and appropriate play.

The other job children have as they are growing up is learning how to act and behave appropriately. Young children learn how to act and behave by testing boundaries, asserting their independence and observing adults and older children. When the children you babysit behave inappropriately, it is your job to guide them to understand how to behave more appropriately.

In this chapter you will learn to recognize which behaviors to expect from children based on their ages and developmental stages, how to handle typical misbehaviors and how to plan safe and appropriate play activities.

Ages, Stages and Milestones

As children grow and develop, their abilities change. Children typically go through certain stages and reach different milestones at predictable ages.

The following chart will help you understand children's physical, social and mental abilities at different ages. It will also help you select and plan safe and appropriate activities.

Remember that this chart lists milestones children *typically* reach at certain ages. No two children are alike, so behaviors and abilities often differ, even among children of the same age. The ages listed are approximate and the stages and milestones will vary from child to child.

Ages, Stages and Milestones

Infant
(Newborn to
12 Months Old)

Toddler
(1 and
2 Years Old)

PHYSICAL
- Gains control of hands—bats, reaches and grasps objects (3 months)
- Rolls over (4 to 6 months)
- Discovers feet—brings feet to mouth and explores with feet (5 months)
- Supports own head (6 months)
- Gets into a sitting position (6 to 8 months)
- Begins rolling, scooting, rocking and bouncing (6 to 8 months)
- Crawls (6 to 9 months)
- Develops pincher grip (thumb and one finger) and begins to hold objects with one hand while manipulating them with the other (6 to 9 months)
- Pulls self up to a standing position (9 to 12 months)
- Moves around by holding on to furniture for support (9 to 12 months)
- Stands alone for 1 or 2 seconds (10 to 12 months)
- Begins to take first steps (12 months)
- Walks alone (10 to 16 months)

PHYSICAL
- Drinks from a cup
- Walks well (younger toddler); runs well (older toddler)
- Is physically active and busy
- Starts potty training (success may vary)
- Dresses self (with lots of supervision and help)
- Feeds self (with hands at first, with small spoon later)
- Washes and dries hands (if able to reach the sink safely)
- Walks up steps but needs help to be safe (by 1½ years)
- Walks down steps but needs help to be safe (by 2 years)
- Strings beads and turns knobs (by 2 years)
- Kicks and catches a large ball (by 2½ years)

SOCIAL
- Shows interest in people, especially faces and voices (2 to 3 months)
- Smiles and laughs at voices and own image in mirror (3 months)
- Talks baby talk or babbles (3 to 4 months)
- Distinguishes among familiar people—has preferences (3 to 4 months)

SOCIAL
- Becomes easily frustrated
- Uses language to express wishes to others
- Has strong desire for independence
- Shows pride in accomplishment
- Relates better to adults than to children but will relate well to other children under adult supervision

SOCIAL continued
- Listens to voices and tries to imitate sounds (5 months)
- Acts shy with new people (6 to 9 months)
- Waves and plays games like peek-a-boo (6 to 9 months)
- Watches and may imitate others (6 to 9 months)
- Recognizes own name (9 months)

SOCIAL continued
- Tries to mimic adults
- Shows affection for others
- Has favorite soft toys or dolls
- Likes being read to and looking at picture books
- Mostly plays alone (under supervision) (until 1½ years)
- Enjoys games like tag (after 1½ years)
- Plays cooperatively with other children (beginning at 2½ years)

MENTAL
- Explores by putting things in mouth (3 months)
- Learns to let go of and drop objects (5 months)
- Remembers people, objects, games and toys (7 months)
- Begins developing interest in picture books (8 months)
- Learns to open and empty cupboards, drawers and other containers (9 months)
- Begins to point to named objects and obey simple commands (9 to 12 months)

MENTAL
- Recognizes and names favorite people and objects
- Shows interest in mechanisms and objects that move or can be moved
- Combines objects with other objects to make simple block structures
- Is very curious; constantly experiments with objects
- Shows interest in hidden-object toys; finds most hidden objects easily
- Is able to sort objects by shape and color
- Identifies objects by pointing, including pictures in a book
- Makes marks on paper and scribbles
- Shows interest in the physical qualities of things—texture, shape, size and color
- Begins to solve problems (by 1½ years)
- Learns to talk (goes from using single words to speaking in simple sentences with a vocabulary of over 50 words by 2 years)

Preschooler (3 and 4 Years Old)

Younger School-Age Child (5, 6 and 7 Years Old)

Older School-Age Child (8, 9 and 10 Years Old)

PHYSICAL

- Has more control of own toilet routine (may wear diaper or training pants at night)
- Washes hands and face
- Takes off shoes, socks and pants; puts on simple clothes
- Dresses, undresses and laces shoes with supervision (by 4 years)
- Runs, jumps, climbs and balances with increased skill
- Likes to take risks and demonstrate physical strength and skill
- Cuts with safety scissors, strings beads and holds a pencil
- Presses buttons on phone keypad
- Catches bouncing ball (can throw a ball overhand by 4 years)
- Rides a tricycle (can ride bike with training wheels by 4 years)

PHYSICAL

- Is becoming more coordinated as arms and legs are growing
- Dresses, bathes (with supervision) and eats on own
- Loses baby teeth; permanent teeth coming in
- Operates electronic devices such as computers, TVs and radios on a regular basis

PHYSICAL

- Increasing weight and height (faster for boys up to 9 years old)
- Growing athletic ability: can throw, kick, bat and swing well
- Ever-increasing dexterity: can shuffle cards and play pick-up sticks

SOCIAL

- Begins to share and take turns
- Is learning the concept of fair play but not ready for competitive play
- Engages in cooperative play with others

SOCIAL

- Becomes aware of sex roles
- Develops growing interest in belonging—enjoys secret languages and passwords

SOCIAL

- Works cooperatively with others
- Plays complex card games—beginning to learn how to lose gracefully

Preschooler (3 and 4 Years Old)	Younger School-Age Child (5, 6 and 7 Years Old)	Older School-Age Child (8, 9 and 10 Years Old)
SOCIAL continued • Understands and knows the difference between what is "mine," "his" and "hers" • Negotiates solutions to conflicts • Is increasingly independent	**SOCIAL continued** • Wants to be liked by and please friends • Prefers to play with children of the same sex • Enjoys group activities—great increase in ability to play cooperatively • Has strong sense of fair play • Begins to follow rules and enjoys games with rules	**SOCIAL continued** • Has interest in clubs and group activities • Plays competitive sports and games • Becomes more independent and self-reliant
MENTAL • Speaks well and asks lots of questions; memory improving • Understands most sentences • Understands counting and knows several numbers • Is able to tell stories (at about 4 years) • Is familiar with common shapes and primary colors • Shows interest in simple number and alphabet play • Is able to copy letters and simple shapes • Is able to make things with construction materials, such as building blocks or construction paper	**MENTAL** • Understands the difference between real and make-believe • Develops interest in nature and simple science • Develops interest in reading, spelling activities and games • Develops interest in simple arithmetic activities and games involving time, calendars and value of coins • Develops interest in the line between fantasy and reality • Learns to tell time • Makes first attempts at learning to play music	**MENTAL** • Plays and carries out activities on own • Thinks critically and independently

Children and Play

Why is Play Important for Children?

Play is an essential part of children's development. Through play children—

- **Develop physically.** Running, jumping, dancing, putting beads on a string and coloring all help children grow.

- **Improve their learning skills.** Learning rhymes, singing songs, doing puzzles, sorting and naming things, counting and reading all help children learn.

- **Understand and control their feelings.** Play-acting, imagining, asking "what if" questions and playing games with others all give children the opportunity to learn about and deal with their feelings.

- **Develop socially.** Following rules, pretending to be someone else, acting out a story, playing team sports, playing an instrument in a band, taking turns jumping rope and playing board games all help improve children's social skills.

How Do Children Play?

There are many types of play, including quiet, creative, active, cooperative, dramatic and manipulative play.

- **Quiet play** helps children calm down. Books, puzzles, dolls, coloring and other activities that involve little physical activity are ways children participate in quiet play.

- **Creative play** gives children the chance to use their imagination through activities such as painting, drawing, music, dance and clay.

- **Active play** allows children to spend their energy. Sports, sand and water play, riding toys, running, climbing and swinging are examples of active play.

- **Cooperative play** means playing with other children and/or adults. During cooperative play, children practice social skills.

- **Dramatic play** involves pretending, often with dolls and action figures, or through activities such as make-believe and role-play.

- In **manipulative play** children make things. Activities such as puzzles, painting, cutting, stringing beads and building blocks are ways children participate in manipulative play.

As children develop and grow older, their interests and the activities they enjoy change. When playing with children, it is important to match the toys and activities with the children's ages and developmental stages. This will help avoid frustration, but more importantly, it will help you keep the children safe. Refer to Chapter 3 for additional suggestions of toys and activities for children of different ages.

Infants (Newborn to 12 Months)

Infants first play by themselves. Older infants play while watching others, but rarely interact directly with others.

Younger infants (newborn to 6 months) enjoy—

- Toys with bright primary colors, high contrasts and simple designs.
- Watching and playing with hanging objects, such as a mobile.
- Soft plush dolls or animals and squeeze toys.
- Play mirrors.
- Having many objects to explore with hands and mouth, such as plastic rings or keys on a ring.
- Looking at books and listening to stories from books.

Older infants (7 to 12 months) enjoy—

- Toys that move and/or make noise.
- Things that can open and shut and contain items.
- Items that can be stacked, poured, pushed or pulled.
- Things that can be squeezed, dropped, poked, twisted or thrown.
- Appearing and disappearing objects.
- Looking at books and listening to stories from books.

Toddlers (1 and 2 Years Old)

Toddlers may play alongside other toddlers, but they rarely share and play with one another. As toddlers develop into preschoolers, they play side-by-side and begin interacting and sharing.

Toddlers enjoy—

- Handling and/or carrying around dolls, stuffed animals and action figures.
- Simple dress-up play.
- Toys that can be pushed, pulled or make noise.
- Playing with toys in pretend scenes that are familiar and realistic such as farms or parking lots.

... that produce effects through a child's manipulation.

... bright colors that look real.

... dumping, pushing, pulling, piling up, knocking down, emptying
... ng things.

... ng off physical skills, such as jumping from heights, climbing,
hanging from arms, rolling, galloping and doing somersaults.

- Arranging things by number, size or other pattern.
- Role-playing with toys and imitating grown-ups.
- Looking at books and listening to stories from books.

Preschoolers (3 and 4 Years Old)

Preschoolers enjoy interacting with one another. Because they are just
beginning to understand fair play, preschoolers sometimes want to make up
their own rules. A game like Duck Duck Goose is perfect for this age group
because it has simple rules and allows children to interact with each other.

Preschoolers enjoy—

- Playing with puppets.
- Making and constructing things.
- Toys with realistic detail and working parts.
- Cars, play scenes and small figures.
- Pretending or playing make-believe.
- Simple board games.
- Physical activities such as running, jumping, climbing, catching, throwing
  and kicking.
- Looking at books and listening to stories from books.

School-Age Children (5 to 10 Years Old)

School-age children learn to play in an organized way. They take on roles,
understand having a leader and play as a team. Rules are very important to
them.

Younger school-age children (5 to 7 years old) enjoy—

- Putting on shows.
- Collecting things and starting hobbies.
- Playing sports, jumping rope and skipping games.
- Dramatic play involving props such as costumes or puppets.
- Games with two or more players.
- Friends.

Older school-age children (8 to 10 years old) enjoy—

- Magic.
- Hobbies.
- Friends.
- Games with many players.
- Sporting and music clubs, teams and lessons.

Why Should You Play with Children?

Playing is fun for both you and the children. It's one of the best parts of the job. When the children are happy and you are all having fun, you know you're doing a good job as a babysitter.

Playing with children makes it easy to supervise them and notice if there are any safety-related problems you need to fix. Playing also gives you the opportunity to model appropriate behavior, control any behavior problems and offer praise for good behavior.

When you are playing with children remember to—

- Respect their likes and dislikes when choosing toys and games. If a child wants to play with an inappropriate toy or game, be sure to explain why he or she cannot play with it.
- Be truly interested and involved.
- Be aware of safety (see "Safety and Toys," pages 56-57).
- Wash your hands and keep toys and play areas clean.
- Cheerfully resolve any problems that arise.
- Enjoy yourself.

Create Play

Directions: *Toys and games do not need to be expensive to be fun. Use pieces of paper, your five senses and household items to create fun games and toys for different ages. Use your imagination and fill in the blanks below!*

Refer to "Children and Play" on pages 64-67 and "Safety and Toys" on pages 56-57 for more ideas.

	Paper	Five Senses	Household Items
Infants	Peek-a-boo using a sheet of paper to hide yourself	Play with toes	Rattle
Toddlers	Play with Chalk	Name colors of common objects	Play in a cardbord box
Preschoolers	Make a paper hat	Smell food	dressup
School-Age Children	Make a paper snowflake	touth	Put on a play with props and costumes

Helping Children Behave

Dealing with difficult behaviors is one of the most common babysitting challenges because, at some point, all children misbehave. Children often need help learning how to control their behavior and how to express themselves. As a babysitter, your responsibilities include trying to prevent misbehavior and dealing with it appropriately when it occurs.

Children misbehave for many reasons. Some of the most common reasons are that the child is—

- Copying the behavior of parents, brothers and sisters or friends.
- Feeling jealous of or competitive toward a sibling.
- Testing limits.
- Asserting independence.
- Tired, frustrated, hungry or scared.
- In need of attention.
- Bored.
- Repeating behavior he or she has been rewarded for in the past.

Encouraging Positive Behavior

Often, by planning ahead, using positive feedback and stepping in early you can encourage positive behavior and prevent misbehaviors. Here are some specific tips you can use to promote positive behavior:

- **Let children know when they are behaving well.** Children respond well to positive reinforcement.
- **Set rules, boundaries and limitations when you first arrive on the job.** Children may not become as upset if they know their boundaries and your expectations beforehand.
  - State your expectations in advance.
  - Do not add extra or unnecessary rules.
  - Keep your expectations realistic and age appropriate; kids will be kids.

- **Create a schedule in advance.** Make it flexible and try to alternate between physical and quiet activities.

- **Follow the normal household routines as closely as possible.** For example, serve dinner at the usual time, have children do their regular chores and allow them to play video games after doing their homework if that is what they typically do.

- **Keep off-limit items out of sight.**

- **Be fair; don't play favorites.**

- **Give children advance notice of approaching changes.** Transitions are difficult for many kids, especially if they involve something the children don't want to do. For example, if bedtime is coming up, say, "Bedtime is in 15 minutes."

- **Try to keep things fun.** Stay positive and enthusiastic. Children will follow your example.

Correcting the Behavior Without Criticizing the Child

When children misbehave, make sure they know that you are unhappy with what they did rather than with them. Children need to know that you won't stop liking them if they misbehave. When you respond to misbehavior, give corrective feedback and use positive and respectful requests to stop or change their misbehavior. Babysitters should **never** shake, slap, spank, lock up, shout at or make fun of children.

When a child misbehaves, you have three choices of how you can respond:

- Do nothing
- Say something
- Physically do something

Each of these methods works best in different situations.

- **Doing nothing** means that you ignore the child's misbehavior if it is safe to do so. Doing nothing works well when a child is misbehaving to get your attention. For example, if a child throws a temper tantrum but is not hurting him- or herself or anyone else, you can ignore the behavior.

- **Saying something** means you tell the child what to do or what not to do. Saying something is the method you will use to solve most common babysitting problems.

  - Stay calm and use a neutral tone even if the child is screaming. Yelling back will only make things worse.

- Explain why the child's behavior is unacceptable.

- Offer an acceptable alternative. If a child really wants to play a video game but it's not allowed, offer to play a card game instead.

- Use "when…then" statements. For example, "When you pick up your toys, then we can read a book."

- **Physically doing something** means that you take physical action to stop the child from misbehaving.

  - Physically stop the child's behavior if it is a physical threat to him- or herself or to others. If the child tries to hit you, then gently, but firmly, grasp the child's arm before he or she can hit you and say, "I won't let you hit me. If you're angry, tell me with words."

  - Change locations. For example, if a child is crying and screaming about not being able to play with his or her skateboard, then try moving inside the house.

  - Physically change the situation. If a child is about to throw a toy, then take the toy away. You can try to divert an infant's or a toddler's attention by presenting a new toy or object.

Consequences

Taking steps to promote positive behavior, as well as taking action when children misbehave, will help you handle most situations. Sometimes you will need to use consequences to help make sure children follow rules. In most cases, you will find out from the parents during the family interview what consequences you should use. In some cases, you may have to come up with a consequence to help you enforce rules.

Consequences should generally be used in the following order:

1. **Natural consequences.**
   Natural consequences are the natural results of an action. For example, you have given a child a piece of cake and said, "Eat the cake at the table or it will fall on the floor. If it falls on the floor, the dog will eat it and you won't have any cake to eat." If the child leaves the table and the cake falls on the floor, the *natural* consequence is that the dog eats the cake that falls on the floor. Only use natural consequences if they are safe and make sure children know them ahead of time.

2. **Logical consequences.**

Logical consequences are those that are closely related to an action. An example of a logical consequence would be if you asked an older sister who knocked over the blocks that her younger brother was playing with to help restack them. Logical consequences only work if they seem to go with the misbehavior.

3. **Withholding privileges.**

Withholding privileges works for school-age children and preschoolers, but may not work for toddlers. If a child does not follow a rule that has been explained to him or her, do not allow him or her to do something he or she enjoys, such as watching television or playing video games.

4. **Time-Out.**

A time-out is a consequence that involves removing a child from a situation and placing him or her in a quiet place for a brief amount of time. If you place a child in a time-out, choose a spot where there are no distractions and make sure you can see him or her at all times. This technique works well for older toddlers and over-excited preschoolers, but avoid using it too much. Give no more than 1 minute of time-out for each year of age. For example, a 4 year old would stay in time-out for no more than 4 minutes.

Common Behavior Challenges

Temper Tantrums

A temper tantrum is a strong outburst of challenging behavior, such as whining, crying, screaming, kicking, hitting or breath-holding. Temper tantrums are common for preschoolers and toddlers as they try to gain more control over their lives. Children this age often lack the language skills to express their feelings and use temper tantrums to show frustration or anger. Temper tantrums often occur when a child is tired, hungry, uncomfortable or trying to get your attention.

NEVER SHAKE AN INFANT OR A CHILD!

Shaking an infant or a child in a moment of frustration or anger can cause serious harm or death. Infants have weak neck muscles and heavy heads, and when an infant is shaken, the head flops back and forth, causing serious damage.

Shaking an infant or a child can cause severe injury, resulting in problems ranging from brain damage to death. Remember, no matter how frustrated or angry you feel, never shake an infant or a child!

Ways to prevent temper tantrums:

- Be flexible.
- Give the children you babysit plenty of positive attention.
- Make sure kids get a lot of physical activity.
- Keep children from getting overly hungry or tired.
- Help children learn to manage their anger.
- Allow children to have some control by giving them choices.
- Distract children before temper tantrums fully develop.
- Create clear ground rules and stick to them.
- Keep off-limit items out of sight.
- Make sure toys and activities are age appropriate.

What to do when children have temper tantrums:

- Do not yell or scream.
- Keep your cool; children can learn from your example.
- Ignore temper tantrums when possible. Make sure children can't hurt themselves or others.
- Listen and try to understand what is upsetting them.
- Encourage children to put their feelings into words.
- Clearly and calmly state the rules.
- Allow children to make a choice between two acceptable solutions.
- Take a break from the situation. For example, try another activity or change locations.
- If necessary, use a time-out.

After children have had a temper tantrum, praise their efforts to gain control of their feelings but do not reward bad behavior. As a babysitter, it is important for you to understand that children are allowed to express their feelings, even angry ones, but it is not okay for children to behave badly when they are angry. Strong emotions are no excuse for bad behavior.

Although older children may stomp or slam a door in anger, school-age children are too old for temper tantrums. If a school-age child is having a temper tantrum, give him or her some time to gain control then try to find out why he or she felt that behavior was necessary. Make a note in your Babysitter's Report Record if school-age children act this way and inform parents when they return.

Crying

Crying is a natural form of expression for infants. In fact, delivery room doctors look for crying as one of the first signs that a newborn is healthy and alert. Crying is an infant's way of communicating everything: pain, hunger, thirst, boredom, discomfort, a soiled diaper, teething, colic and over stimulation.

It's also natural for babies to cry, even when nothing is wrong, just to expend excess energy and begin to interact with their environment. If you plan to babysit infants, get used to crying. A normal infant cries 1 to 3 hours each day!

BREATH-HOLDING

Some children purposely hold their breath when they are having a temper tantrum as a way to gain control over the situation. A child who holds his or her breath on purpose is not in danger and this behavior should be ignored. However, some children may have a medical condition known as breath-holding spells.

Children who have breath-holding spells may momentarily stop breathing in some stressful situations. During a breath-holding spell, a child's face may turn deep blue and the child may pass out then quickly regain consciousness. Sometimes children will twitch and jerk during a breath-holding spell.

Breath-holding spells—

- Are an involuntary reflex; children cannot prevent them from happening.

- Happen when children are crying and/or may be part of a temper tantrum.

If you know that the child you are babysitting has breath-holding spells, then during a spell, have the child lay flat on the floor or the ground. If one is available, put a wet washcloth on the child's forehead until he or she starts breathing. Be careful that the child does not injure him- or herself if the child falls. Do not put anything in the child's mouth. After the spell, briefly comfort the child and continue with the activity that was occurring prior to the breath-holding spell.

If the child you are babysitting begins holding his or her breath and is not known to have breath-holding spells, care for the conditions you find.

The best way to handle most crying episodes is to respond quickly and try to meet the infant's basic needs. When an infant cries, you should first check to see that his or her basic needs are met:

- Is the infant hungry?
- Is the infant tired?
- Does the infant need a diaper change?
- Is the infant too hot or too cold?
    - For excessive crying in infants due to cold, dress the infant warmly or adjust the temperature. However, be sure the baby doesn't get too hot. Be especially careful that the baby is not too hot when he or she is sleeping to decrease the risk of sudden infant death syndrome (SIDS). Refer to page 92 for important information on SIDS.
    - If you feel too hot or cold, chances are the infant feels the same way.

If the baby's basic needs are met, but the crying continues, check the baby from toe-to-head for possible causes of pain or discomfort, such as diaper rash, injuries or fever.

Sometimes, you won't be able to determine why an infant is crying. The following techniques can help calm a crying baby:

- **Gentle Motions**
    - Holding the infant in your arms, gently rock back and forth while standing or sitting in a rocking chair.
    - Walk while holding the infant in your arms.
    - Push the infant in a stroller or carriage.
    - Dance quietly with the infant using gentle up-and-down, back-and-forth and side-to-side motions.
- **Soothing Sounds**
    - Position the infant so he or she can hear—
        - A loudly ticking clock.
        - Running or dripping water from a faucet or shower.
        - A running vacuum cleaner.
        - A fan or air conditioner.
        - A metronome set at 60 beats per minute.
        - A tape recording of waterfalls or ocean waves.
        - A running dishwasher or washing machine.
        - Lullabies.

- Classical music.
- Tape recordings of the baby's own cry.
- **Visual Delights and Distractions**
  - Position the infant so that he or she can see—
    - Ceiling lights or chandeliers.
    - The swinging pendulum of a grandfather clock.
    - A revolving ceiling fan.
    - An aquarium.
    - Running water.
    - Leaves on trees.

COLIC

Colic is a condition in which an otherwise healthy baby cries more than 3 hours a day, for more than 3 days a week, between the ages of 3 weeks and 3 months. The crying usually starts suddenly at about the same time each day. Colic generally starts to improve at about 6 weeks and is generally gone by the time a baby is 12 weeks old.

Intestinal gas, food sensitivity or allergy or an immature nervous system may cause colic. A baby with colic may have a red face and a tense, hard belly because the stomach muscles tighten during crying. A baby with colic may also clench his or her legs, feet and fists when crying.

A colicky infant can be a challenge for even the most experienced babysitter. Be sure to ask the parents if their infant has colic before you agree to babysit.

The following holds can relax a colicky infant:

- **The arm drape (also called the football hold).** Rest the baby's head in the crook of your elbow. Drape the baby's stomach along your forearm and grasp the diaper area firmly. Your forearm will press against the baby's tense stomach. When the baby's arms and legs dangle, the baby is beginning to relax.

- **Colic curls.** Babies who tense their tummies and arch their backs often settle in this position. Slide the baby's back down your chest and encircle your arms under his or her bottom. Curl the baby up, facing forward with the head and back resting against your chest. To help relieve gas, try pumping the baby's thighs in a bicycle motion.

- ○ Moving cars.
- ○ The movement of a mechanical metronome.
- ○ Children playing.
- ○ Pets playing.
- ○ Changing images on TV.

Biting, Hitting and Kicking

Biting, hitting and kicking are common behaviors for toddlers and younger preschoolers. At this age, they may not know that these behaviors are wrong and can hurt someone. Children this age also don't always know how to use words to express anger or frustration. Sometimes children bite, hit or kick to get your attention or when they are hungry, thirsty or tired. It is important not to overreact when the children you babysit act this way.

If a child bites, hits or kicks—

- ○ Assess the situation before you react.
- ○ Encourage the child to explain the problem in his or her own words.
- ○ Explain appropriate behavior. For example, say, "It's not okay to hit people when you're mad. If you are mad because your brother took your toy, politely ask him if you can have it back."
- ○ Ask questions aimed at giving the child an understanding of the victim's perspective. For example, say, "Has anyone ever bitten you?"
- ○ Comfort the child who was hurt before you deal with the child who did the hurting.
- ○ Change activities or locations. Certain toys, activities or locations may cause children to become frustrated.
- ○ Try taking a break for a snack, drink, nap or bedtime.
- ○ Do not bite back children who bite. This models inappropriate behavior and may reinforce further biting.
- ○ If a child continues this behavior, then provide a consequence such as withholding a privilege or using a time-out.

The best way to deal with biting, hitting and kicking is to try to prevent it in the first place. The following techniques will help you prevent these behaviors.

- ○ Try to recognize and reinforce children's attempts at using their words to get your attention or to solve problems before biting, hitting or kicking occurs.
- ○ Help children use words to express frustration when it begins. For example, tell a child to say, "Please may I have it back" when an older sibling takes a toy away.
- ○ Use age-appropriate toys to discourage frustration.

- Establish clear rules and boundaries before starting an activity.
- Have enough toys for all children.
- Alternate quiet- and high-energy activities to prevent over excitement.
- Stick to normal routines.
- Keep items that may cause frustration out of sight.
- Make sure the children get enough of your attention.

Children older than 5 years should not bite, hit or kick. Make a note in your Babysitter's Report Record if school-age children behave this way and inform parents when they return. For information about children who bite, hit or kick when fighting with siblings, see "Sibling Rivalry."

Sibling Rivalry

Sibling rivalry is the jealousy, competition and fighting that breaks out between brothers or sisters (siblings) over everything from toys to attention. Sibling rivalry is common and can even start while a mother is still pregnant with her second child. It is not unusual for siblings to swing back and forth from fighting to getting along well with each other.

Though it may be hard to believe, sibling rivalry can even have a positive side. Working things out with their siblings gives children a chance to

ADHD

Attention Deficit Hyperactivity Disorder (ADHD) is a special condition diagnosed by doctors for children with an especially hard time paying attention or controlling their behavior. Children with ADHD might forget where they put things, fidget or even interrupt when someone else is talking because of this condition. If you babysit for a child with ADHD, the parents will likely have special instructions that you should follow.

ADHD Facts

- 8 percent to 10 percent of all children have ADHD.
- ADHD begins during preschool years.
- Boys are more likely to have ADHD than girls.
- Children with ADHD may need extra help learning to do things other children find easy.

Source: "What is Hyperactivity" from *www.KidsHealth.org*

develop important skills like getting along with others and being able to see another person's point of view.

The following factors add to sibling rivalry:

- Children who are trying to establish their individuality may compete with a sibling.
- Children who feel they are getting unequal amounts of attention, discipline and responsiveness may act out towards a sibling.
- Children who are hungry, bored or tired are more likely to start fights.
- Children may not know positive ways to get attention from their brother or sister, so they pick fights.
- Stress in children's lives can create more conflict.

Whenever possible, try not to get involved in sibling rivalries; however, stop dangerous fights immediately. If you have to step in, solve the problem **with** the siblings, not **for** them. Follow these tips:

- Separate kids until they're calm.
- Don't yell or lecture.
- Don't put too much focus on figuring out which child is to blame.
- If the children are extremely angry, then have them leave the room to calm down. When they are calm, encourage them to talk things out.
- Encourage win-win negotiations, where each side gains something.
- Establish ground rules (basic rules for how to act towards each other) for solving arguments, such as—
  - No hurting.
  - No name-calling, yelling or tattling.
  - If you are fighting over a toy, the toy will be taken away.
- Involve children in setting ground rules.
- Remember that things don't have to be fair and equal. Sometimes one child needs more than the other. For example, an older child may be allowed to play with a certain toy because it is appropriate for his or her age even if the younger sibling wants to play with the same toy too.

The following can help prevent fights or arguments between siblings:

- Set rules with clear and consistent consequences.
- Plan activities that are fun for everyone.
- Make sure each child has enough time and space of his or her own.
- Don't play favorites.
- Select activities that encourage cooperation rather than competition.
- Never compare children.
- Have fun together.
- Give all kids one-on-one attention.

BABYSITTING FOR MILITARY FAMILIES

In most ways, military families are no different than other families. What is special about military families is that a parent—and sometimes both parents—may be gone for long periods of time, often in distant, dangerous or unknown locations. This is called deployment. Deployment can be a stressful time for military families.

Some children whose parents have been deployed may not seem to be bothered, while other children may experience fear, worry, doubt, confusion, sadness, anger and/or guilt. The stress of deployment may cause some children to act differently than they normally would act. Common reactions include:

- Infants: May refuse to eat or seem less active.

- Toddlers: May be gloomy, cry, have tantrums, have trouble sleeping or feel irritable and sad.

- Preschoolers: May regress in skills, have potty accidents, act clingy or feel irritable and sad.

- Younger and Older School-Age Children: May whine or complain more than usual, have trouble sleeping, lose interest in school, experience body aches or feel irritable and sad. Some children may become more aggressive. While some children might want to be left alone, it is important for children this age to spend time with people talking about their feelings and to stick to normal routines.

Here's how you can help when you are babysitting for military families:

- Maintain regular routines.

- Give children extra attention, comfort (holding and hugging) and reassurance.

- Be patient and calm when children are clingy, whiny and aggressive.

- If possible, answer any questions about deployment with brief, to-the-point responses to avoid children's imaginations from taking over.

- Let children know that their parents are doing an important job.

FIND Decision-Making Model Activity

Directions: *Practice using the **FIND** decision-making model by filling in the blanks below after watching the scenario.*

The Case of the Babysitter and the Bouncing Boys

F

Figure out the problem.

The Kids are supoose to go to bed but they are jumping on the Bed

I

Identify possible solutions.

If you Stop I will read you a story

N

Name pros and cons for each solution.

+ you gould get hurt
- I will caly your parnets

D

Decide which solution is best, then act on it.

you could get hurt so I suggest you stop Jumping

CHAPTER 5

From Feeding to Bedtime: Caring for Kids

Caring for kids is the heart of babysitting.

In this chapter, you will learn how to give basic child care and how to keep germs from spreading while you are doing so. You will also learn about the importance of care routines and how to model good basic child-care behavior.

Talking to the Parents About Basic Child Care

Effective basic child care begins with understanding the family's routines for care. Child-care practices, routines, supplies and equipment vary among families, so it is always important to ask parents about their preferences. For example, some parents use disposable diapers, some use cloth; some children always have a bath and story before bed, others like their stories on the living room sofa and are only bathed by their parents. Children are usually happier if you stick to their basic child-care routines.

Gather all the information about basic child care that you will need to know before you babysit. Write down any basic child-care instructions on the Family Interview Form, found on the *Babysitter's Training CD-ROM.* Report to the parents about the basic child care you provided when they return. Use the Babysitter's Report Record, found on the *Babysitter's Training CD-ROM.*

Watching Out for Germs

While on the job, you could come into contact with germs. Germs can be transmitted by—

- Direct contact with other people's body fluids, such as blood and saliva.
- Air, when breathing in droplets from someone else's cough or sneeze.
- Contact with an object or surface that has been in contact with a germ, such as a telephone.
- An insect, animal or human bite.

Some germs can cause you to catch a cold or the flu or expose you to common childhood diseases like chicken pox. Other germs can cause serious diseases, like the human immunodeficiency virus (HIV), the virus that causes acquired immunodeficiency syndrome (AIDS).

The most important steps you can take to stay healthy and avoid the spread of germs are to wash your hands often and wear disposable gloves if there is a chance you could come into contact with blood or other body fluids such as urine or vomit.

Hand Washing

Hand washing is the best way to prevent the spread of germs and infectious diseases.

Always wash your hands—

- Before and after you prepare food.
- Before and after you eat.
- Before and after changing diapers or helping a child with toileting.
- After using the toilet.
- After playing outdoors.
- After touching insects, plants or pets.
- After cleaning up spills.
- Before and after giving first aid.
- After coughing, sneezing or blowing your nose.

ALCOHOL-BASED HAND SANITIZERS

Alcohol-based hand sanitizers are a good alternative to washing your hands with soap and water. You can use alcohol-based hand sanitizers if there is no water available and your hands are not visibly dirty (i.e., your hands don't have dirt or blood on them). To use alcohol-based hand sanitizers follow these steps:

1. Apply alcohol-based hand sanitizer to the palm of one hand, using the amount recommended by the manufacturer.

2. Rub hands together making sure to cover all surfaces of your hands and fingers until they are dry.

Remember to always keep alcohol-based hand sanitizers out of the reach of children.

Make sure children wash their hands—

- Before and after they eat.
- After using the toilet (wash infants' hands after they are diapered).
- After touching objects or surfaces used by other people in public areas.
- After playing outdoors.
- After coughing, sneezing or blowing their noses.
- After touching or handling insects, plants or pets.

For step-by-step instructions on washing your hands, see the Skill Sheet, found on pages 93-94.

Wearing Disposable Gloves

Wear disposable gloves if you could come into contact with blood or other body fluids. Many families will not have disposable gloves available, so make sure you take some with you. The babysitter's first aid kit contains nonlatex disposable gloves, and you can also buy them at supermarkets and drugstores. Be sure to find out in advance whether any children you will be caring for are allergic to latex. While many disposable gloves are made from latex, it is best to get gloves that are nonlatex, such as vinyl or nitrile.

Use a new pair of disposable gloves—

- When you change a diaper.
- When you give first aid.
- When you touch any body fluids.

As a babysitter, it is important to use disposable gloves to limit contact with blood, urine, feces or vomit. This will reduce the possibility that you will become infected with infectious diseases. Be sure to carefully remove and properly dispose of gloves after using them. When you remove gloves, be careful not to get any body fluids on yourself. Wash your hands before giving care as well as when you are finished giving care and have disposed of your gloves. For step-by-step instructions on removing disposable gloves, see the Skill Sheet found on pages 95-96.

Picking Up and Holding Children

Most children enjoy being held, although some do not. Respect individual preferences. Remember to ask parents how their children like to be picked up and held during the family interview. Write down their answers on the Family Interview Form.

Infants

There are several ways to hold an infant. These include the cradle hold, which is used for feeding an infant, and the shoulder hold, which works well if you are walking with a baby or trying to calm a baby down. Always remember to support the head, neck and back of infants under 6 months old. Also, for many infants, holding them close to your body makes them feel safe and secure.

Toddlers

Here are some tips on picking up and holding toddlers:

- Toddlers like to be held and carried, but only do so if you can support their weight and their parents say this is okay.
- You can hold toddlers on your lap when giving them a bottle or a drink from a spill-proof cup or when reading to them.
- Toddlers may climb off your lap if they want to play or if they see something they want to investigate, so pay close attention.
- Ask toddlers to help when you need to carry them. They can put both arms around your neck to hold on securely.
- When picking up a toddler, bend at your knees and lift. Don't bend your back. Also remember to pick them up in a smooth and continuous motion.
- After picking up a toddler, use the upright carry to move him or her from one place to another in an upright position.

For step-by-step instructions on picking up and holding infants and toddlers, see the Skill Sheets found on pages 97-100.

Feeding Children

Be sure to ask parents about when, what and how much to feed their children. Pay special attention to what kinds of snacks they are allowed and when they can have them. Write down their instructions on the Family Interview Form. Keep the following tips in mind when feeding children.

Bottle-Feeding

- Infants and toddlers may drink milk, formula, fruit juices or water from a bottle.
- When feeding an infant from a bottle you will need a bottle, nipple, bib or cloth to protect the infant's clothing and a towel or cloth to put over your shoulder for burping.

- **NEVER** warm a bottle in a microwave. Instead, warm the bottle until it is lukewarm (not hot) by running it under warm faucet water or placing it in a pot or bowl of hot water. After heating the water, turn off the heat source and remove the pot from the heat source. Place the bottle in the pot or bowl to warm. Watch the bottle carefully; leave it in the water for a few minutes. Check the temperature of the bottle often to be sure it doesn't become too hot. Realize that if it is too warm to you, it may be too hot for the child.

- **ALWAYS** test the temperature before giving a bottle to a child or an infant. Drip a small amount of the liquid onto the inside of your wrist to make sure it's cool enough. To avoid the spread of germs, do not touch the nipple to your skin. A lukewarm bottle will not burn a child's mouth.

Spoon-Feeding Older Infants and Toddlers

- When feeding older infants and toddlers with a spoon you will need a dish, the food, an infant or toddler spoon and a bib. Ask parents what supplies they would like you to use when feeding their children. Write down their answers on the Family Interview Form.

- You can warm food by putting the container of food into hot water. If you use a microwave to heat the food, be sure to stir the food well and to test the temperature before giving it to an infant or a toddler. Put a small amount of food on the inside of your wrist to make sure it's cool enough. Be careful to not touch the spoon to your wrist. Lukewarm food won't burn a child's mouth.

- Don't blow on food to cool it. Let it cool by itself.

- Infants who are just beginning to eat from a spoon may seem to be pushing the food away. Be patient and keep feeding them as long as they seem interested.

- Let toddlers try to feed themselves with a spoon or their hands if they want, even if they make a mess. Help toddlers as needed.

Feeding Preschoolers and School-Age Children

- Most young children eat with their fingers, although some will use a small fork or spoon. Eating is fun for most children. Don't worry if they are messy, you can always clean them up.

- If a child does not eat much or refuses to eat or drink, wait a few minutes and try again. If the child is playing with the food more than eating, he or she is probably finished.

- Older children can feed themselves, but you will need to prepare their food. Let them pitch in by helping you set the table.

For step-by-step instructions on feeding children and infants, see the Skill Sheets found on pages 101-104.

Food and Kitchen Safety

- Wash your hands before you prepare food.
- Wash raw fruits and vegetables carefully before eating them or feeding them to children.
- Be careful when using a microwave. Stir food well after removing it from the microwave.
- Always test the temperature of food and drinks before giving them to children.
- Never leave a child alone in any type of chair even for a moment and even if he or she is strapped into the chair.
- Keep high chairs away from stoves and counters.
- Always use the safety straps on high chairs and booster seats to secure children.
- If you must use the stove, make sure young children are in a safe place where you can see them, approximately 3 feet from the stove. Use only the back or rear burners and turn pan handles toward the back of the stove, out of the reach of children.
- Don't let children play in the kitchen.
- Follow the parents' directions for cleaning up and putting away unfinished food and drinks.
- Avoid foods that are choking hazards for infants or toddlers such as raisins, popcorn, nuts, hard candy, grapes and hotdog slices. Make sure food is cut into small bite-size pieces.

Diapering

When diapering, it is always good to remember the following:

- Some infants or toddlers are easier to change if they have a toy to hold. Be sure to get the toy before you start diapering.
- Always clean from the front to the back and separate the folds of skin to ensure cleanliness.

For step-by-step instructions on diapering, see the Skill Sheet found on pages 105-107.

Tearless Toileting Tips

Some older toddlers and most preschoolers are learning to use the toilet. Follow the parents' routine and ask what words or signals their children will use to tell you that they need to use the bathroom. Write down their answers on the Family Interview Form.

Here are some tips for tearless toileting:

- Wash your hands before and after helping a child use the toilet. Be sure children wash their hands after toileting.

- Some children use a child-size toilet or a seat that fits on top of the regular toilet. Other children use the regular toilet seat. Be certain you know what they are comfortable with.

- Children who are already toilet trained sometimes still need help unfastening their clothes, wiping themselves or washing their hands. If you help a girl with wiping, wipe from front to back to keep from spreading germs. Be sure girls who don't need your help know that they should wipe themselves from front to back.

- Never make a big deal out of an accident because it might embarrass the child. Clean the child and say it was a good try. Be sure to wear disposable gloves when cleaning the child.

- Encourage children to use the toilet often. Give children an opportunity to use the toilet before and after eating, sleeping and activities such as playing outside. If children are showing signs that they need to use the bathroom, such as clutching at their pants, shivering or jumping around, take them to the bathroom immediately.

Dressing Children

Ask the parents if they want you to dress their children and if they have any special instructions. Write their answers on the Family Interview Form. Dressing should be easy and safe if you keep the following tips in mind:

- Give yourself enough time to change the children. Rushing makes the job more difficult and can upset children.

- Let toddlers help with dressing by encouraging them to pull off their socks or pull a loose shirt over their heads. Let them help you undo snaps or buttons.

- Be sure to keep infants safe and comfortable. Never leave an infant alone on a changing table, bed or sofa.

- Don't let children walk around on uncarpeted surfaces in socks without skid-proof bottoms.
- To help prevent children from tripping, do not dress them in pants that are too long. If pants are too long, be sure to roll up the pant legs. Make sure shoes fit securely and laces are tied.
- Avoid dressing children in clothes that fasten with drawstrings, especially around the neck. A child can be strangled by a hooded sweatshirt when a drawstring tie catches on something.

For step-by-step instructions on dressing children, see the Skill Sheets found on pages 108-110.

Bathing Toddlers

Bath time can be fun, but remember that safety always comes first and the child requires constant supervision. If you're asked by the parents to bathe their toddler, ask them about the child's bath time routine. Make sure to ask about the child's favorite shampoo, soap and toys and any sensitivities. ***Remember, only bathe toddlers if you've specifically been asked to by their parents and you are comfortable doing so.*** Babysitters should not bathe infants.

When giving a bath, always keep safety in mind. Remember these important points:

- Never be more than an arm's length away from the toddler at any time.
- Never take your eyes off the toddler during bath time. This includes when you are filling up the bath tub and when it is draining.
- If you are caring for more than one child, only give a bath if you can supervise all the children adequately (e.g., you are babysitting two children and the younger school-age child can play independently next to you).
- Gather all supplies and toys before you run the water.
- Don't fill the tub too high. The water only needs to come up to the toddler's hips.
- The water should be warm, but not hot. Test the water on your wrist or elbow before putting the child in the tub.
- Be aware of the sharp edges of the faucet and keep the child's head away from it.
- Remember that the tub will be slippery. Always help the child in and out of the bath and make sure the toddler stays seated while in the tub.
- Never force a child to take a bath.

- Bath time should be fun and not hurried. Let the toddler get accustomed to the bath before you start washing or shampooing. Also, give the toddler time to play.

- Tilt the child's head back when you shampoo and rinse his or her hair. Remember that some children are very sensitive to water on their face. If toddlers resist having their hair washed, do not force them.

Rest and Sleep

Families have a wide variety of rest and sleep routines. Ask the parents about the child's nap, rest and bedtime routines. Write their answers on the Family Interview Form.

Some children wake up or come out of quiet time in a calm way. Other children wake up noisy and ready to play. Some children wake up crying or upset.

Putting Children to Bed

Follow these steps when you are putting children to bed:

1. Ask parents about their children's bedtime routines and record their answers on the Family Interview Form.

2. About 15 minutes ahead of time, tell children that bedtime or naptime is coming.

3. Anticipate requests by making sure to follow the children's normal bedtime routines. Typical routines include having a bedtime drink or snack, brushing teeth, reading a story or book, turning on a nightlight, bringing a stuffed animal to bed or using a favorite blanket.

4. Help prepare children for sleep by choosing quiet activities such as reading comforting stories, listening to soft music or rubbing the child's back.

5. Check an infant's crib and remove toys, blankets, pillows or any other soft, fluffy objects that could choke or suffocate the infant. (See the Safety Inspection Checklist , found on pages 36-37, for more bedtime safety tips.)

6. Put infants to sleep on their backs, face-up. It is not safe for infants to sleep on their stomachs or face-down. (See "Sudden Infant Death Syndrome," found on page 92) Some parents may request that you put their infants to sleep on their sides. You should do so only if a parent tells you

that a doctor has directed that the infant sleep this way and the parent shows you how to correctly position the infant on his or her side.

7. Tell the child to sleep well and say good night.

8. Check on children every half hour. Make sure you stay where you are able to hear them when they wake up. Discuss with the parents how to use the baby monitors if they have them. Write down their instructions on the Family Interview Form.

9. Put children back to bed if they get up. Comfort them if they are scared or have nightmares. Be kind but firm in helping children follow their rest and sleep routines.

SUDDEN INFANT DEATH SYNDROME (SIDS)

Sudden Infant Death Syndrome (SIDS) is the sudden, unexpected and unexplained death of an apparently healthy infant. It is the leading cause of death of infants between the ages of 1 month and 1 year. In the United States, 3000 infants die every year of SIDS. Infants who sleep on their stomachs at night or naptime have an increased risk of SIDS.

To help reduce the risk of SIDS—

- **ALWAYS** place an infant on his or her back at night or naptime, using a firm mattress in a safety-approved crib or bassinet.

- Make sure that there is no soft bedding, such as pillows, blankets and bumpers, or soft toys, such as stuffed animals, in the crib or bed. These items could cause suffocation.

- Check the sleeping infant frequently.

Hand Washing

NOTE: *Remove all jewelry and watches.*

1 Turn on warm water.

2 Wet your hands with water and put soap on your hands.

3 Rub your hands together for at least 15 seconds (about the time it takes to sing "Happy Birthday" once) (A).

NOTE: Scrub your nails by rubbing them against the palms of your hands (B).

4 Rinse your hands with water.

5 Dry your hands with a paper towel.

6 Turn off the faucet using the paper towel. Throw the paper towel away.

NOTE: Use alcohol-based hand sanitizers to clean your hands if hand-washing facilities are not available.

Removing Disposable Gloves

 Partially remove the first glove.
- Pinch the glove at the wrist, being careful to touch only the glove's outside surface (A).

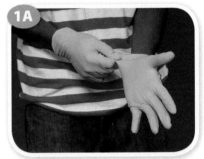

- Pull the glove inside-out toward the fingertips without completely removing it (B).
- The glove is now partly inside-out.

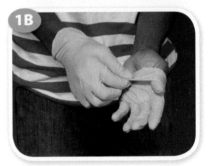

Remove the second glove.
- With your partially gloved hand, pinch the outside surface of the second glove.
- Pull the second glove toward the fingertips until it is inside-out, and then remove it completely.

Finish removing both gloves.

- Grasp both gloves with your free hand.
- Touch only the clean interior surface of the glove.

After removing both gloves—

- Discard gloves in an appropriate container.
- Wash your hands thoroughly.

Picking Up Infants

NOTE: Always support the head, neck and back of an infant younger than 6 months old.

 Slide both of your hands under the infant's underarms.

Wrap your fingers around the infant's ribs.

Gently lift the infant while supporting his or her head with your fingers.

OR

Slide one hand under the infant's head and back.

 Slide your other hand under the infant's bottom.

Gently lift the infant while supporting his or her head.

Holding Infants: Cradle Hold

NOTE: *Always support the head, neck and back of an infant younger than 6 months old.*

1. Support the infant's bottom and lower back with one hand.

2. Cradle the infant in your arm and support the upper back and head with your other arm.

3. Hold the infant's head near or at the bend of your elbow.

4. Hold the infant close to your body with the infant's back straight and protected.

Holding Infants: Shoulder Hold

NOTE: Always support the head, neck and back of an infant younger than 6 months old.

1   Put one arm under the infant's bottom and support the head and back with the other arm.

2   Hold the infant in an upright position so that he or she can look over your shoulder.

Picking Up and Holding Toddlers: Upright Carry

1 Bend your knees.

2 Pick up the toddler under both arms. Slide both of your hands under the toddler's underarms and lift.

3 Put one arm under the toddler's bottom and support his or her back with your other arm.

TIP: Use your hip to help support the arm placed under the toddler's bottom.

Bottle-Feeding

1 Wash your hands.

2 Gather supplies.

3 Warm and prepare the bottle as the parent directed.

NOTE: *Shake the bottle to make sure it is heated evenly. Test the temperature on the inside of your wrist; it should be lukewarm (not hot).*

4 Rest the infant comfortably on your lap.

NOTE: *Keep the infant's head higher than his or her shoulders to prevent choking.*

5 Give the infant the bottle.

NOTE: Hold the bottle for the infant. Tilt the bottle to a 45-degree angle so that air is not getting into the nipple.

6 Gently burp the infant when he or she has taken about one third of the bottle.

NOTE: Hold the infant upright and put his or her head on your shoulder. Pat the infant gently on the back until you hear a burp.

TIP: You can also burp the infant by sitting him or her on your lap, making sure you support his or her head, and patting gently on the back.

7 After burping the infant, give the remainder of the bottle. Burp the infant again when he or she is finished drinking.

Spoon-Feeding

1 Wash your hands and the child's hands.

2 Gather supplies.

3 Warm and prepare the food as the parent directed.

NOTE: Stir food to make sure it is heated evenly. Test the temperature on the inside of your wrist; it should be lukewarm (not hot).

4 Put the child in a high chair or infant seat. Buckle the safety belt securely.

5 Put a small amount of strained food or cereal on the tip of the spoon and feed the child.

6 When you are done feeding, wash the child's hands and face and wipe up any food that was spilled.

7 Wash your hands.

Diapering

1 Gather supplies.

2 Wash your hands.

3 Put on disposable gloves.

NOTE: *Use the safety straps or guardrails on a changing table to secure the infant or toddler.* **Never** *leave an infant or a toddler alone on a changing table. Keep one hand on the infant or toddler at all times. Use a changing table or the floor protected with a water-resistant pad to change the infant or toddler.*

4 Place the infant or toddler on his or her back.

5 Take off the dirty diaper.

Cloth Diapers: Remove rubber pants first, then unfasten and remove pins from the diaper. DO NOT put the pins in your mouth.

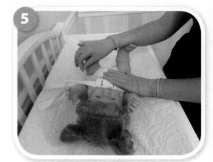

NOTE: *Fold the diaper so that the mess is on the inside. Set the dirty diaper out of the way where the infant or toddler can't reach it.*

6 Use one hand to hold the infant's or toddler's feet and lift up the bottom, then clean with baby wipes or a washcloth.

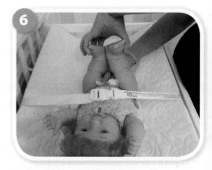

TIP: *Keep boys and girls covered with a baby wipe or a diaper while changing them to avoid being sprayed.*

7 Use one hand to hold the infant's or toddler's feet and lift up the bottom. Use the other hand to slip the open clean diaper under his or her bottom.

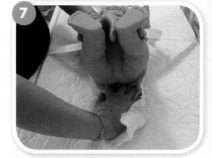

Cloth Diapers: Put the clean diaper under the infant or toddler with the folded part in front for a boy and in the back for a girl.

8 Fasten the diaper with the tabs.

Cloth Diapers: Overlap the back of the diaper on top of the front at the infant's or toddler's hips. Hold your fingers between the diaper and the infant or toddler and pin on the outside of the diaper.

NOTE: *Put your fingers between the diaper and the infant or toddler so that you do not tape or pin the diaper to him or her.*

9 Remove your disposable gloves and dispose of them, the dirty diaper and baby wipes in an appropriate container.

Cloth Diapers: Dispose of the feces in the toilet and put the dirty diaper in the appropriate container.

NOTE: *Keep one hand on the infant or toddler at all times. Make sure the changing surface is clean.*

10 Wash the infant's or toddler's hands and place him or her in a safe place while you wash your hands.

Undressing Children

 Undo the snaps or buttons on the front of the shirt.

 Gently slide one arm out of the sleeve and then slide out the other arm.

 Ease the shirt over the child's head, gently past one ear, then the other.

NOTE: *When undressing an infant, always support the head and neck. Never leave an infant alone on the changing table.*

 Put the dirty laundry in the place designated by the parents.

Dressing Children in Snap or Button Shirts

1 Open all snaps or buttons.

2 Roll or scrunch-up the sleeves if they are long.

3 Reach through one sleeve, grasp the child's hand and pull the hand and arm gently through the sleeve.

4 Bring the shirt around the back of the child. Do the same with the other arm.

5 Fasten the snaps or buttons.

Dressing Children in a T-Shirt

 To put on a T-shirt or pullover shirt, stretch the neck of the shirt so that it is larger than the child's head.

 Pull the neck opening over the head, keeping it away from the child's ears and face.

 Reach through a sleeve opening and gently pull one arm through it.

Do the same with the other arm.

NOTE: *Always be careful to protect the child's eyes, ears, nose and jaw.*

CHAPTER 6

It's an Emergency... Now What?

Babysitters must know how to recognize an emergency and what to do if one takes place.

In this chapter, you will learn how to recognize an emergency, how to tell the difference between life-threatening and nonlife-threatening emergencies and how to react when an emergency occurs.

What Is an Emergency?

An emergency is a situation in which action is needed right away. Some emergencies involve calling 9-1-1 or the local emergency number, and some do not. The most important thing to do in any emergency is to stay calm.

How Do You Know It's an Emergency?

A babysitter needs to use his or her senses of sight, smell, touch and hearing to determine if there is an emergency. To recognize an emergency, use your senses and pay attention to—

- Unusual sights.
- Unusual noises (silence can also be an unusual "noise" with children).
- Unusual odors (or smells).
- Unusual appearances or behaviors.
- Anything a child tells you, such as "I have a stomachache" or "I don't feel well."

These signals could mean that you need to take action quickly to protect yourself and the children.

What Is a Weather Emergency?

Weather emergencies, such as a flood or tornado, require your immediate action. You may need to call for help or get the children to a safe place.

What Are Some Other Emergencies?

Other emergencies, such as fires, explosions or violence, also require you to take action. Again, you may need to call for help or get the children to a safe place.

What Is a First Aid Emergency?

A first aid emergency involves an injury or sudden illness. All first aid emergencies require your immediate action. Some involve calling 9-1-1 or the local emergency number; others do not. For example, a small cut on a child's finger requires your prompt action, not a call to 9-1-1; however, for a life-threatening first aid emergency, such as a child who is not breathing, you need to call 9-1-1 or the local emergency number.

Life-Threatening Emergencies

Life-threatening emergencies are situations that could cause death quickly if you do not take immediate action. In a life-threatening emergency, you need to call 9-1-1 or your local emergency number. The following are life-threatening emergencies:

- A child or an infant who is unconscious. An unconscious child or infant will not be able to respond to your taps and shouts. Tapping a child's or an infant's shoulder or flicking the bottom of an infant's foot plus shouting, "Are you okay?" should cause a reaction, such as crying or movement, in a child or an infant who is simply sleeping.
- A child or an infant who is having trouble breathing.
- A child or an infant who has no signs of life (movement or breathing).
- A child or an infant who has no pulse (heartbeat).
- A child or an infant who is bleeding severely.

For any life-threatening emergency, call 9-1-1 or the local emergency number. If someone is with you who knows how to call 9-1-1, have him or her call while you give care.

In a First Aid Emergency:
CHECK—CALL—CARE

If you find yourself in a first aid emergency, stay calm and follow three basic emergency action steps: **CHECK—CALL—CARE**

CHECK

Check the scene:

- Make sure there is nothing that could hurt you or cause further injury to the child. If there is, get yourself and the child to a safe place.
- Look for any clues that may show what happened. For example, you might see some broken glass that could have caused an injury or an open bottle of cleaning solution that could have poisoned a child.

Check the child or infant:

- See what is wrong. Tap the child or infant (also flick the infant's foot) and shout to see if he or she is awake, then check for life-threatening emergencies (see Checking a Conscious Child or Infant Skill Sheet, found on pages 132-134, or Checking an Unconscious Child or Infant Skill Sheet, found on pages 137-138).

CALL

- In a life-threatening emergency, call 9-1-1 or the local emergency number. If someone is with you, such as a child old enough to use the telephone, have him or her call while you give care.

- If the problem is not life threatening, call the parents as soon as possible to let them know what happened.

CARE

- The care you give will depend on the kind of emergency or problem you find.

- This handbook will help you learn how to handle different types of emergencies. The emergency reference guide will help you *quickly find* the information you need to take care of the different kinds of injuries and illnesses children or infants may experience.

Calling for Help

Call 9-1-1 or the local emergency number.

Write your local emergency number here: _____

NOTE: *Remember to find out the local emergency number for each family you babysit and write it down on the Family Information Card.*

The National Poison Control Center (PCC) hotline is: (800) 222-1222.

How to Call for Help

1. Call 9-1-1 or the local emergency number.

2. Tell the dispatcher, or call taker, who answers the phone that you have a medical, fire or police emergency.

3. Answer any questions you are asked, such as who you are; what happened; what is the address (and nearest cross-street); the number you are calling from; how many people are injured; and what type of care, if any, is being given.

4. Don't hang up! Wait until the dispatcher tells you to hang up. He or she may need more

information. The dispatcher might tell you what to do. Follow his or her instructions. The dispatcher will send medical help to your location to give care. An ambulance may arrive first or police or firefighters may come to help if they can get there first.

5. After you call 9-1-1 or the local emergency number, return to the child or infant and continue care until EMS personnel arrive. After EMS personnel arrive and take over, call the child's parents and tell them what happened.

When You're Alone: Call First or Care First?

If you are alone and the child or infant is unconscious (that is, he or she does not respond to your taps and shouts), you will have to decide if you should start by calling for help or giving care. The following Call First or Care First guide will help you to determine what to do first.

○ **CALL FIRST**, that is, call 9-1-1 or the local emergency number before giving care for—

  ○ A person who is about 12 years old or older and is unconscious.

  ○ A child or an infant who you see suddenly collapse.

  ○ An unconscious child or infant who you know has heart problems.

○ **CARE FIRST**, that is, give 2 minutes of care before calling 9-1-1 or the local emergency number for—

  ○ An unconscious child younger than about 12 years old who you did not see collapse.

  ○ Any victim of a drowning.

In most cases, you will **Care First** for a child or an infant who is unconscious since the cause is most likely to be a breathing emergency and not a cardiac (heart) emergency. For an unconscious adult or adolescent (about 12 years old or older), however, you will generally **Call First** because adults and adolescents are more likely to suffer from cardiac emergencies. In this case, the focus is on calling 9-1-1 or the local emergency number first to get emergency medical services (EMS) personnel on the scene as quickly as possible.

REMEMBER: *If you are in an emergency situation and not sure what to do, call 9-1-1. The dispatcher will send help and may tell you what to do.*

FIRST AID KIT

A first aid kit should contain the items that you will need for an emergency. You can make your own or buy a Babysitting Essentials Kit. Always take your first aid kit with you when you babysit. Make sure your first aid kit has the supplies you need and it is ready to use. If you take the children away from home, such as to the park or for a walk, take the kit with you. Always let the parents know where you are going.

Keep the first aid kit away from the children. Some things in the kit can be dangerous for them. If you do not have a first aid kit, ask where the family's first aid kit is located when you are interviewing the parents. Ask to see the kit and check it out to make sure it has the supplies you might need.

Any first aid kit should include at a minimum the following:

- Disposable nonlatex gloves (two pairs)
- Alcohol-based hand sanitizers (for use when soap and water are not available)
- Adhesive bandages in different sizes and shapes (kids like the colored ones and those with pictures)
- Sterile gauze pads
- Roller gauze bandages
- Emergency numbers and Family Information Card
- Adhesive tape
- Safety scissors
- Tweezers
- CPR breathing barriers for giving rescue breaths
- Cold pack

Additional items may include:

- Notepad
- Pen or pencil
- Small battery-powered flashlight
- Zipper-lock plastic bags (for ice packs)
- Mobile phone or change for a pay phone
- Anything else specifically needed for the children you are babysitting

Keep your emergency reference guide in your kit.

Checking a Conscious Child or Infant

If a child or an infant is injured or suddenly becomes ill and he or she is conscious, you will need to check him or her from toe-to-head. Checking in this order gives the child a chance to get used to the process and allows him or her to see what is going on.

Begin by observing the child or infant before you touch him or her. Look for signals that something is wrong. Get at eye level with the child. As you conduct your check, speak slowly and in a friendly manner. Using simple words, ask questions about what happened in a way that the child can easily answer. A young child or an infant may not be able to verbally respond to your questions, but he or she may be able to point or use other nonverbal cues to tell you what is wrong.

For step-by-step instructions on checking a conscious child or infant, see the Checking a Conscious Child or Infant Skill Sheet, found on pages 132-134.

Checking a Conscious Child

Directions: *Answer the following questions as you watch the video segment, "Checking a Conscious Child."*

1. What is the first thing you should do when you arrive at the scene to check a conscious child?

2. What should you look for when checking toe-to-head?

3. When you check the child's arms, what should you ask him or her to do?

4. How should you check skin color and temperature?

5. When should you call 9-1-1 or the local emergency number?

What Is a Breathing Emergency?

A breathing emergency is when someone is not breathing or is having trouble breathing. If a child or an infant has a breathing emergency, you must act fast. The heart will stop soon if the child or infant is not breathing. First aid for a breathing emergency can save a child's or an infant's life.

Breathing emergencies can occur for different reasons, such as—

- An asthma attack.
- An allergic reaction to a bee sting or other substance.
- An electric shock or drowning that causes breathing to stop.
- Choking on an object, such as a piece of food or a small toy.
- An illness, such as croup, that causes a swollen throat.

Signals of a Breathing Emergency

The signals of a breathing emergency include a child or an infant who—

- Is unable to relax or be still.
- Is upset or agitated.
- Is sleepy.
- Is dizzy.
- Has pale, blue or ashen (gray) skin color.
- Has blue lips or fingernails.
- Has unusually fast or slow breathing.
- Has noisy breathing including wheezing, gurgling or whistling.
- Has hoarse crying or coughing in a way that sounds like barking.
- Is grasping at the throat.
- Cannot cough, cry, speak or breathe.
- Has a surprised, confused or panicked look, which may be accompanied by silence.
- Exhibits breathing where you can see the muscles between the ribs going in and out.

Check Out the Problem

If the child or infant is coughing, crying or speaking, he or she is conscious and breathing but still may be having trouble breathing. Some children and infants have problems that affect their breathing, such as asthma or allergies. The parents should tell you about these types of during your family interview. They should also give you [instructi]ons that tell you what to do in case of an asthma attack or [allergic] reaction. Follow the parents' instructions. Call 9-1-1 or your local emergency number if the breathing is fast or slow or the child or infant is pale or blue. To help a child or an infant who is having trouble breathing, see the following:

- "Allergic Reactions," in the emergency reference guide, pages 6-7
- "Asthma Attack," in the emergency reference guide, pages 7-8
- Conscious Choking—Child Skill Sheet, page 135
- Conscious Choking—Infant Skill Sheet, page 136
- Checking an Unconscious Child or Infant Skill Sheet, pages 137-138
- Rescue Breathing—Child or Infant Skill Sheet, page 139
- Unconscious Choking—Child or Infant Skill Sheet, page 161-162

Asthma

Asthma is an ongoing illness in which airways (small tubes in the lungs through which we breathe) have ongoing swelling. An asthma attack occurs when a trigger, such as exercise, cold air, allergens or another irritant, affects the airways causing them to suddenly swell and narrow. This makes breathing difficult.

Triggers of an Asthma Attack

A trigger is anything that sets off or starts an asthma attack. Asthma triggers include (but are not limited to)—

- Dust, smoke and air pollution.
- Fear or anxiety.
- Hard exercise.
- Plants and molds.
- Perfume.
- Colds.
- Medications.
- Animal fur or feathers.
- Temperature extremes and changes in the weather.

Signals of an Asthma Attack

- Coughing or wheezing
- Trouble breathing
- Shortness of breath
- Rapid shallow breathing
- Inability to talk without stopping for a breath
- Tightness in the chest
- Feeling of fear or confusion
- Sweating

For more information on how to care for an asthma attack, go to pages 7-8 in the emergency reference guide.

Choking

Choking is a common breathing problem in children and infants. A choking child or infant can quickly stop breathing, become unconscious and die. That's why it is important to be able to tell when a child or an infant is choking.

Signals of Choking

A child or an infant may be choking if he or she is—

- Coughing hard but can't get the object out of the airway.
- Coughing weakly or making a high-pitched sound while breathing.
- Unable to cough, cry, speak or breathe.
- Clutching or grabbing at the throat.
- Unconscious and a responder cannot get the chest to rise with the first 2 rescue breaths.

Care for Choking

If the child or infant is coughing forcefully, encourage him or her to keep coughing. If a child or an infant cannot cough, cry, speak or breathe, however, then he or she is choking and needs immediate care. The care you give a child who is conscious and choking is a combination of back blows (strikes between the shoulder blades) and abdominal thrusts (thrusts just above the belly button). For an infant, you will give a combination of back blows and chest thrusts.

The care you give a child or an infant who is unconscious and choking (cannot get the chest to clearly rise after two attempts to give 2 rescue breaths) is similar to cardiopulmonary resuscitation (CPR) except that you look to see if there is an object and remove it between the compressions and breaths. There are also differences between how you care for a child and an infant because their body sizes are different. You will learn more about each skill later in this chapter and the next chapter.

See the following to learn more:

- Conscious Choking—Child Skill Sheet, page 135
- Conscious Choking—Infant Skill Sheet, page 136
- Unconscious Choking—Child or Infant Skill Sheet, pages 161-162

CPR BREATHING BARRIERS

You may feel uncomfortable putting your mouth on someone else's to give rescue breaths, especially if it is someone you don't know. While it's normal to worry about this, the chance of getting a disease from giving rescue breaths is very low. Using a CPR breathing barrier can lower that risk even more.

A CPR breathing barrier is a piece of equipment used to protect you from coming into contact with a person's blood and other body fluids. There are several types of CPR breathing barriers, including face shields and resuscitation masks. They come in various sizes to fit the faces of adults, children or infants.

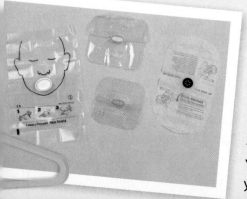

If you have a face shield, be sure to learn how to use it. Some simple face shields are small enough to fit in your pocket or first aid kit. Place this shield over the child's or infant's mouth and nose and then breathe through the opening.

Keep a CPR breathing barrier in your first aid kit or ask if the family has one. Be sure to learn how to use it. Always follow the manufacturer's instructions. You can buy CPR breathing barriers at your local Red Cross chapter.

Unconscious Children and Infants

If someone is unconscious, it is a life-threatening emergency. If you come upon a child or an infant who appears to be motionless, you must act quickly.

Checking an Unconscious Child or Infant

Any time a child or an infant is not moving, you need to check for life-threatening conditions, such as—

- Unconsciousness.
- Trouble breathing.
- No signs of life (movement or breathing).
- No pulse.
- Severe bleeding.

To check an unconscious child or infant, follow the steps on the Checking an Unconscious Child or Infant Skill Sheet, found on pages 137-138.

Checking a Child's or an Infant's Pulse

If an unconscious child or infant shows no signs of life (movement or breathing) and the first 2 rescue breaths go in, check for a pulse for no more than 10 seconds. For a child, check the carotid pulse by placing your

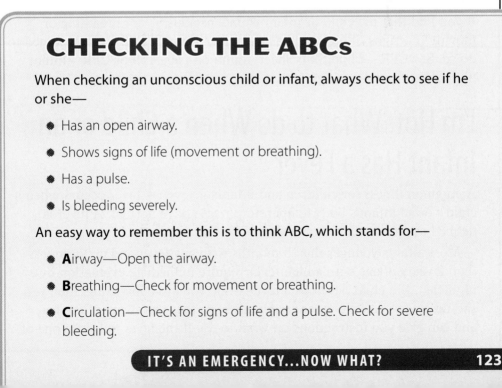

CHECKING THE ABCs

When checking an unconscious child or infant, always check to see if he or she—

- Has an open airway.
- Shows signs of life (movement or breathing).
- Has a pulse.
- Is bleeding severely.

An easy way to remember this is to think ABC, which stands for—

- **A**irway—Open the airway.
- **B**reathing—Check for movement or breathing.
- **C**irculation—Check for signs of life and a pulse. Check for severe bleeding.

fingers on the middle of the throat and sliding your fingers into the groove on the neck. For an infant, check for a brachial pulse by pressing your first two fingers against the bone on the inside of the infant's upper arm between the elbow and the shoulder.

Caring for an Unconscious Child or Infant

If you find that the child or infant is unconscious, the care that you give will depend on the additional conditions that you find during your check.

Child or Infant is Unconscious and Breathing

If you find that the child or infant is unconscious and breathing, place him or her in a recovery position while you call 9-1-1 or the local emergency number. See the Checking an Unconscious Child or Infant Skill Sheet, found on pages 137-138.

Child or Infant is Unconscious, Not Breathing, but Has a Pulse

If you find that the child or infant is unconscious, is not breathing or moving (no signs of life) but has a pulse, give rescue breathing. See the Rescue Breathing—Child or Infant Skill Sheet, found on page 139.

Child or Infant is Unconscious, No Signs of Life And No Pulse

If you find that the child or infant is unconscious, is not breathing or moving (no signs of life) and has no pulse, begin CPR if you are trained to do so. See CPR—Child Skill Sheet, found on page 159 or CPR—Infant Skill Sheet, found on page 160.

I'm Hot: What to do When a Child or an Infant Has a Fever

A common illness for children and infants is fever. A fever occurs when a child's or an infant's body temperature rises above normal. A fever is defined as a temperature of 100.4° F (38° C) or greater.

Most infants younger than 3 months with any fever and children less than 2 years of age with a high fever require immediate evaluation by a physician. If a child develops a fever while you are babysitting, then you should always call the parents right away so they are aware of the fever and can give you instructions on what to do. If the fever falls into one of

RECOVERY POSITIONS

If you need to leave an unconscious child or infant for any reason, such as to call for help, you will need to place the child or infant in a recovery position. This position helps the airway remain open and clear if the child or infant vomits.

There are two kinds of recovery positions. Figure 6-1 shows the position used for a child or an infant who you do not think has a head, neck or back injury.

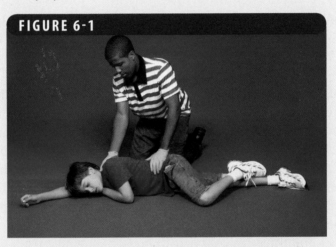

FIGURE 6-1

Figure 6-2 shows the recovery position to use if you think the child or infant has a head, neck or back injury. For this position, you will need to move the child or infant to his or her side while keeping the head, neck and back in a straight line. This position is called the modified High Arm in Endangered Spine (H.A.IN.E.S.) recovery position.

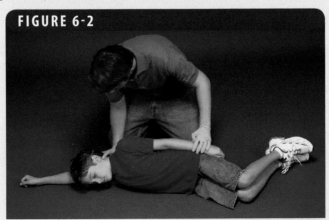

FIGURE 6-2

the categories of concern listed above, then the parents should contact the child's physician about what to do and they should come home right away. You should also call the parents if you are not able to take a child's or an infant's temperature and he or she feels warm.

Taking a Child's or an Infant's Temperature

During the family interview, make sure to ask the parents what method and what type of thermometer they prefer you to use to take their child's or infant's temperature. You should also ask them to show you how to use the thermometer. Always ask for the parents' permission before taking a child's temperature.

A rectal temperature (in the rectum) is the recommended method for taking the temperature of children under age 5. For children age 5 and above, an oral temperature (in the mouth) is the recommended method. You may also take an oral temperature for children age 3 and up.

Although a rectal temperature gives the most reliable reading for children under 5, do not use this method if the parents do not want you to or if the child becomes upset or uncooperative when you attempt to do so. In addition to rectal and oral methods, two other options for taking a child's temperature include using the tympanic (in the ear) (if the equipment is available) or axillary (under the arm) method. The tympanic method should be used as the first option. If a tympanic temperature cannot be taken, then use the axillary method.

There are multiple types of thermometers available. Whenever possible, use an electronic (digital) thermometer to take a temperature. Also, use a manufacturer's thermometer that is specifically designed for the type of temperature being taken (for example, only use a tympanic thermometer for taking a child's temperature in the ear). Read the manufacturer's directions carefully so you know how to use the thermometer appropriately.

When taking a temperature, follow these safety guidelines—

- Always stay with a child while taking a temperature to ensure the child does not move, so the thermometer does not break and/or cause injury.
- Do not use an oral thermometer to take a rectal temperature.
- Only use a tympanic thermometer to take a temperature in the ear.
- Gather all supplies before beginning to take a temperature.
- To prevent disease transmission, wash your hands before and after taking a temperature and wear disposable gloves.
- Do not use a glass or mercury thermometer. If possible, always use an electronic (or digital) thermometer.

Which Thermometer to Use and When

Preferred Method	Age	Alternate Methods	Notes
Rectal (in the rectum)	*Under* age 5	If parents do not want you to use rectal method, or child or infant is upset or uncooperative: Tympanic (in the ear) if equipment is available; OR Axillary (under the arm)	Rectal method should only be used on children *under* 5 years of age. Use rectal method *only if parents approve.* *Do not* use an oral thermometer to take a rectal temperature.
Oral (in the mouth)	*Over* age 5	Tympanic (in the ear) if equipment is available; OR Axillary (under the arm)	May also be used for children age 3 and older. *Do not* use an oral thermometer to take a rectal temperature.

How to Take a Temperature

NOTE: Use disposable gloves and other equipment to protect against disease transmission.

NOTE: When taking a temperature, always follow manufacturer's and parents' instructions for the thermometer being used.

1. Gather supplies.
2. Check to make sure the equipment is working.
3. Turn the thermometer on.
4. Position the child or infant appropriately.

5. Take a temperature.

For Oral (Mouth) Temperature

- Put the thermometer under the child's tongue and slightly to one side.
- Ask the child to close his or her lips and not to bite down on the thermometer with his or her teeth.
- Always stay with the child while you are taking an oral temperature.

For Rectal (Rectum) Temperature

NOTE: This method should only be used on children under 5 years old.

- Put a small amount of lubricating jelly on a tissue.
- Apply lubricating jelly to the tip of the thermometer from the tissue.
- Put the child or infant on his or her stomach on a hard surface.
- Put one of your hands on the child's or infant's lower back, right above the bottom. Using the other hand place the thermometer into the anal opening. DO NOT place the thermometer farther than 1 inch.
- Keep the thermometer in place by holding it with two fingers.
- Always stay with the child while you are taking a rectal temperature.

For Tympanic (Ear) Temperature

- Ask the child or infant to turn his or her head so the ear is in front of you.
- Pull up and back on the ear to straighten the ear canal.
- Gently insert the probe into the ear.
- Always stay with the child while you are taking a tympanic temperature.

For Axillary (Under Arm) Temperature

- Uncover the child's or infant's underarm area and dry it with a tissue if necessary.
- Put the thermometer in the middle of the child's or infant's underarm.
- Bring the child's or infant's arm across the chest to hold the thermometer in place.
- Make sure the child or infant is sitting or lying down during the process and not walking around with the thermometer under his or her arm.
- Always stay with the child while you are taking an axillary temperature.

6. Read the number on the thermometer.

7. Follow the manufacturer's instructions for cleaning the thermometer.

8. Remove gloves and dispose of them in the appropriate container and wash your hands.

If the Child or Infant Has a Fever

Remember, if the child or infant has a fever, call the parents and tell them what is happening. For more information on what to do if a child or an infant has a fever, see pages 32-33 in the emergency reference guide.

Bleeding Emergencies

Children and infants get scrapes and scratches frequently. Wounds and injuries bleed when blood vessels under the skin are torn or damaged.

If the bleeding stops quickly and there is very little blood, then it is considered minor bleeding. When minor bleeding occurs, follow the care steps for Minor Bleeding, found on pages 12-14 in the emergency reference guide.

With a more serious wound or injury, like a deep cut, severe bleeding may occur and be hard to stop. Blood can squirt from a wound if a larger blood vessel under the skin is damaged. In this case, first aid is needed right away to stop the bleeding. The Controlling External Bleeding Skill Sheet, found on page 140, tells you how to care for severe bleeding.

Types of Wounds

The first aid you give will depend on the type of wound. These include—

- ○ **Scrapes (Abrasions).** This type of wound is the most common (Fig. 6-3). The skin is rubbed or scraped away, often from a fall. Usually these wounds do not bleed a lot, but they need careful cleaning to prevent infection.

FIGURE 6-3

○ **Cuts (Lacerations).** This type of wound can be caused by sharp objects, such as scissors, knives or broken glass (Fig. 6-4). These wounds sometimes cause a lot of bleeding.

FIGURE 6-4

○ **Avulsions or Amputations.** With this type of wound some of the skin and sometimes other soft tissue is partially or completely torn away. When a body part is completely torn away, including the bone, it is called an amputation. These wounds can cause a lot of bleeding especially if the skin or body part has been completely torn away.

○ **Puncture.** This type of wound happens when a pointed object, such as a nail, needle or a knife, pierces deep through the skin (Fig. 6-5). These wounds may bleed very little and may become infected.

FIGURE 6-5

Burns

Another type of wound is a burn. Burns are caused by heat (thermal), chemicals, electricity and the sun (radiation). Burns can damage one or more layers of skin and the layers of fat, muscles and bone beneath. Burns are classified by their depth. The deeper the burn, the more severe it is. The three levels of burns are superficial (first degree), partial thickness (second degree) and full thickness (third degree). A burn can appear red, brown, black or white and it may swell and be painful. Deep burns can range from very painful to almost painless.

Call 9-1-1 or the local emergency number for critical burns. Critical burns include those that—

- Involve the head, neck, mouth or nose or cause trouble breathing.
- Are to a child or an infant (other than very minor ones).
- Cover more than one body part or large surface area.
- Are to the hands, feet or genitals.
- Result from chemicals, explosions or electricity.

When a burn occurs, follow the care steps for Burns, found on pages 18-20 in the emergency reference guide.

Checking a Conscious Child or Infant

NOTE: Use disposable gloves and other equipment to protect against disease transmission.

CHECK the scene for safety. **CHECK** the child or infant.
CALL 9-1-1 for any life-threatening emergencies.

1 Ask—

- What happened?
- Are you having any trouble breathing?
- Are you in pain?
- Where are you hurt?

NOTE: Do not ask the child or infant to move any areas that hurt. Do not ask the child or infant to move if you think there is an injury to the head, neck or back. Note pain, discomfort or if he or she is unable to move.

2 Check toe-to-head for—

- Bleeding, cuts, bruises and obvious deformities.
- Medical ID bracelets and necklaces.

3 Check the feet, legs and hips one at a time.

4 Check the arms one at a time. Ask him or her to—
- Move the hands and fingers.
- Bend the arms.

5 Check the stomach and chest. Ask him or her to—
- Take a deep breath and blow air out.
- Tell you if he or she is experiencing pain during breathing.

6 Check the shoulders. Ask him or her to—
- Shrug the shoulders.

7 Check the neck.
- If there is no pain and you do not suspect a head, neck or back injury, ask if he or she is able to move the head slowly from side to side.

8 Check the head.
- Look at the scalp, face, ears, eyes, nose and mouth for cuts, bumps, bruises and depressions.
- Notice if he or she is alert, drowsy or confused.

Check skin color and temperature.
- Feel the forehead with the back of your hand.
- Look at the face and lips.

CARE for any conditions you find.

NOTE: *If the child or infant can move all body parts without pain or discomfort and has no signals of life-threatening emergencies—*

- *Have him or her rest for a few minutes in a sitting position.*
- *Help him or her to SLOWLY stand when he or she is ready.*
- *Pick up and comfort the child or infant if there are no signals of an injury.*

Conscious Choking—Child

CHECK the scene. **CHECK** the child. CANNOT COUGH, SPEAK OR BREATHE—**CALL** 9-1-1.

NOTE: Depending on the child's size, you may have to kneel.

1. Lean the child forward and give 5 back blows with the heel of your hand between the shoulder blades.

2. Give 5 quick, upward abdominal thrusts (A, B).

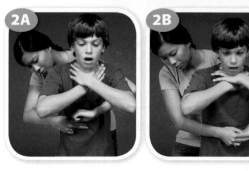

3. Continue back blows and abdominal thrusts until the—
   - Object is forced out.
   - Child can cough forcefully, speak or breathe.
   - Child becomes unconscious.

NOTE: If the child becomes unconscious, lower him or her gently to the floor. CALL 9-1-1, if the call has not already been made, and give care for unconscious choking if trained to do so.

Conscious Choking— Infant

CHECK the scene. **CHECK** the infant. CANNOT COUGH, CRY OR BREATHE—
CALL 9-1-1.

1 Give 5 back blows.

2 Give 5 chest thrusts.

*NOTE: Hold the head and neck securely when giving
back blows and chest thrusts.*

3 Continue back blows and chest thrusts
until the—
- Object is forced out.
- Infant can cough forcefully, cry or
breathe.
- Infant becomes unconscious.

*NOTE: If the infant becomes unconscious, **CALL** 9-1-1, if the call has not already been
made, and give care for unconscious choking if trained to do so.*

Checking an Unconscious Child or Infant

NOTE: Use disposable gloves and other equipment to protect against disease transmission.

CHECK the scene. **CHECK** the child or infant.

1. Tap shoulder and shout, "Are you okay?" (A)
   - For infant, also flick foot (B).

2. No response, **CALL** 9-1-1.
   If alone—
   - Give about 2 minutes of **CARE**.
   - Then **CALL** 9-1-1.

   If response, GO TO Checking a Conscious Child or Infant.

NOTE: If an unconscious child or infant is face-down, roll the child or infant face-up while supporting the head, neck and back.

3. Open airway (tilt head, lift chin), **CHECK** for signs of life (movement and breathing) for no more than 10 seconds.

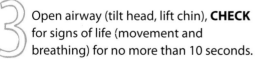

4 If no breathing, give 2 rescue breaths.

5 If breaths go in, **CHECK** for pulse and quickly scan for severe bleeding (A, B).

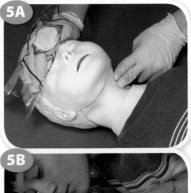

6 If the child or infant is or starts breathing on his or her own, place in recovery position and monitor ABCs.

WHAT TO DO NEXT

IF BREATHS DO NOT GO IN—Give care for unconscious choking if trained to do so.

IF PULSE, BUT NO BREATHING—Give rescue breathing.

OR

IF NO SIGNS OF LIFE AND NO PULSE—Give CPR or use an AED (if an AED is immediately available) if trained to do so.

Rescue Breathing—Child or Infant

NOTE: Use disposable gloves and other equipment to protect against disease transmission.

CHECK the scene. **CHECK** the child or infant. IF PULSE, BUT NO BREATHING— **CALL** 9-1-1.

1. Give 1 rescue breath about every 3 seconds.

   For Child—
   - Pinch nose shut.
   - Make seal over child's mouth.
   - Blow in to make chest clearly rise.

   For Infant—
   - Seal mouth over infant's mouth and nose.
   - Blow in to make chest clearly rise.

2. After about 2 minutes, recheck signs of life and pulse for no more than 10 seconds.

WHAT TO DO NEXT

IF PULSE, BUT NO BREATHING—Continue rescue breathing.

IF NO SIGNS OF LIFE AND NO PULSE—Give CPR or use an AED (if an AED is immediately available) if you are trained to do so.

Controlling External Bleeding

NOTE: Use disposable gloves and other equipment to protect against disease transmission.

CHECK the scene. **CHECK** the child or infant.

1. Cover wound with a sterile dressing.

2. Apply direct pressure until bleeding stops.

3. Cover the dressing with a roller bandage.

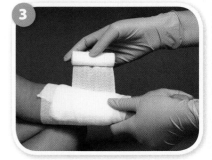

4. If bleeding does not stop—
   - Apply additional dressings and bandages and apply more pressure.
   - Take steps to minimize shock.
   - **CALL** 9-1-1 if not already done.

NOTE: Wash hands with soap and water after giving care.

CHAPTER 7

First Aid, CPR and AED

Learning first aid and CPR are critical skills for a babysitter.

In Chapter 6, you learned how to recognize an emergency and how to react when one occurs. In this chapter, you will learn additional first aid skills, as well as the lifesaving skill of cardiopulmonary resuscitation (CPR).

Good Samaritan Laws

Most states have Good Samaritan laws that protect people who voluntarily give emergency care to an injured or ill person without accepting anything in return. These laws, which differ from state to state, usually protect you from legal liability (lawsuits) as long as you—

- Act in good faith.
- Are not negligent or reckless on purpose. Negligence is the failure to act or acting beyond your training and your action causes further harm.
- Do not do anything that you have not been trained to do.
- Do not abandon the person after starting to give care.

You should contact a legal professional or check the local library to find out more about your state's Good Samaritan laws.

Obtaining Consent

Before giving first aid to a person who is alert and able to respond, you must ask if it is okay for you to give care. This is referred to as getting consent. A conscious adult has the right to either tell you that it is okay or not okay for you to give care.

In general, to get consent you must—

1. Give your name.
2. Tell the person or his or her parent or guardian that you are trained in first aid.
3. Ask the person if you may help.
4. Explain what you think may be wrong.
5. Explain what you plan to do.

Important points to remember:

- **DO NOT** give care to a conscious adult who says it is not okay for you to give care.
- If a person does not give consent, call 9-1-1 or the local emergency number.

If the conscious person is a child or an infant, ask the parent or guardian if it is okay for you to give care if he or she is present. If a parent or guardian is not present, consent is implied. Implied consent means you can assume that if the parent or guardian were there, he or she would tell you it is okay to give care to their child or infant. During the family interview, you should get permission from the parents to give care to their children if they get injured or become ill while you are babysitting. You do not need to get consent from the children. If you give any type of care, remember to notify a parent or guardian as soon as possible.

Recognizing and Caring for Shock

Shock is a life-threatening condition in which not enough blood is being delivered to all parts of the body and, as a result, body systems and organs begin to fail. A child or an infant showing signals of shock needs immediate medical attention. Shock is likely to develop after any serious injury or illness, such as severe bleeding, serious internal injury, significant fluid loss or other conditions. The goal of first aid is to get help quickly and give care to reduce the effects of shock while caring for the injury or illness.

PERMISSION FOR BABYSITTERS

When you interview parents before a babysitting job, be sure to let the parents know your level of first aid training and ask for their permission in advance to care for any injuries or illnesses that may arise. You should also have the parents fill out and sign the Parental Consent and Contact form, found on the *Babysitter's Training CD-ROM*, which gives hospitals permission to give care if the parents cannot be contacted. Ask the parents if the child or infant has any medical conditions that you should be aware of, including allergies, and if there are special steps that you should follow. If the parents want you to give the child any medications, have them show you exactly how to do so. Note all instructions on the Parental Consent and Contact Form.

It is always best to get permission from the parents to care for any injuries or illnesses that may arise; however, even if you haven't received permission from the parents, you should still give care. In this type of situation, permission is implied. If you have not asked for the parents' permission to give care or you are unsure of what to do, you can always call 9-1-1 or the local emergency number. Be sure to call the parents to tell them about the injury or illness and any care that was given as soon as possible.

Once the parents have granted permission for you to give care to their child or infant, it is not necessary for you to ask the child or infant for permission to give care at the time of the injury or illness; however, you should consider the child's or infant's feelings when giving care. Remain calm and reassure the child or infant. Let him or her know that you are going to help and what you are going to do.

Signals of Shock

Signals that a child or an infant may be going into shock include—

- Being restless or easily annoyed or bothered.
- Changed (or changing) level of consciousness.
- Nausea or vomiting.
- Rapid breathing and pulse.
- Pale or gray, cool, moist skin.
- Being very thirsty.

Care for Shock

- Make sure that 9-1-1 or the local emergency number has been called.
- Continue to closely watch the child's or infant's ABCs (airway, breathing and circulation).
- Control any external bleeding.
- Keep the child or infant from getting chilled or overheated.
- Raise the legs about 12 inches if you don't think the child or infant has a head, neck or back injury or if you don't think the child or infant has any broken bones in the hips or legs. If unsure, leave him or her lying flat.
- Comfort and reassure the child or infant until emergency medical services (EMS) personnel arrive and take over.

Do not give the child or infant anything to eat or drink, even though he or she is likely to be thirsty. The child's or infant's condition may be serious enough to require surgery, in which case it is better if the stomach is empty.

Moving a Child or an Infant
"Do No Further Harm"

One of the most dangerous threats to a seriously injured child or infant is unnecessary movement. Usually when giving care, you will not face dangers that require you to move a child or an infant.

Moving a seriously injured child or infant can cause additional injury and pain and make the recovery more difficult. You should move a child or an infant only in the following three situations:

1. When you are faced with immediate danger, such as fire
2. When you have to get to another person who may have a more serious injury or illness
3. When you need to move the child or infant to give proper care

If you must move the child or infant for one of these reasons, you must quickly decide how to move him or her. Carefully consider your safety and the safety of the child or infant.

To avoid hurting yourself or the child or infant, use your legs, not your back, when you bend. Bend at the knees and hips and avoid twisting your body. Walk forward when possible, taking small steps and looking where you are going.

Avoid twisting or bending anyone who you think has a possible head, neck or back injury. Do not move a child who is too large to move comfortably.

Emergency Moves

There are many ways to move a child or an infant. Some work better in certain situations than others.

Walking Assist

To help a child who needs help walking to safety—

1. Place the child's arm around your shoulders or waist, depending on the child's size, and hold it in place with one hand.

2. Support the child with your other hand around the child's waist (Fig. 7-1).

3. Move the child to safety.

Another person, if present, can support the child in the same way on the other side.

FIGURE 7-1

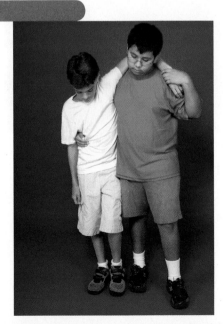

Pack-Strap Carry

To move either a conscious or an unconscious child who you **do not** think has a head, neck or back injury—

1. Position yourself in front of the child, with your back to the child's front.
2. Place the child's arms over your shoulders and cross them in front of your neck and then grasp the child's wrists.
3. Lean forward slightly and pull the child onto your back (Fig. 7-2). To do this, you may have to kneel close to the ground. Then, when you lift, use the power in your legs to get up and move.
4. Move the child to safety.

FIGURE 7-2

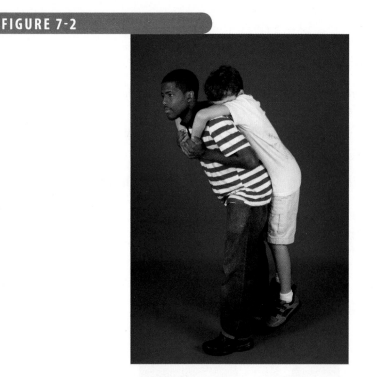

Two-Person Seat Carry

To carry a child who cannot walk and who you **do not** think has a head, neck or back injury—

1. Put one arm under the child's thighs and the other across the child's back, under his or her arms.
2. Interlock your arms with another person's arms under the child's legs and across the child's back.

3. Lift the child in the "seat" formed by your interlocked arms (Fig. 7-3).

4. Move the child to safety.

FIGURE 7-3

Clothes Drag

To move a child or an infant who may have a head, neck or back injury—

1. Gather the child's or infant's clothing behind his or her neck.

2. Pull the child or infant to safety (Fig. 7-4).

   ○ While moving the child or infant, cradle the head with his or her clothes and your hands.

FIGURE 7-4

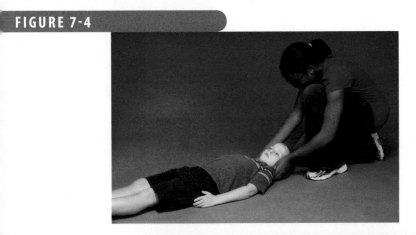

Blanket Drag

To move a child in an emergency situation when equipment is limited—

1. Keep the child between you and the blanket.
2. Gather half the blanket and place it against the child's side.
3. Roll the child toward you as a unit.
4. Reach over and place the blanket so that it will be positioned under the child.
5. Roll the child onto the blanket.
6. Gather the blanket at the head and move the child to safety (Fig. 7-5).

FIGURE 7-5

Foot Drag

To move a child who is too large to carry or move otherwise—

FIGURE 7-6

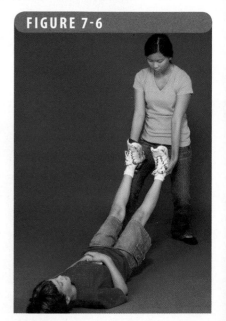

1. Firmly grasp the child's ankles and move backward (Fig. 7-6).
2. Pull the child in a straight line and be careful not to bump his or her head.

The Cardiac Chain of Survival

Cardiac arrest is the condition in which the heart stops working altogether. CPR alone is not enough to help someone survive cardiac arrest. Emergency medical care is needed as soon as possible. This is why it is so important to call 9-1-1 or the local emergency number immediately. Although rare, children and teenagers can experience cardiac arrest.

The greatest chance of survival from cardiac arrest occurs when the following things happen one after the other as rapidly as possible:

1. **Early recognition and early access.** The sooner 9-1-1 or the local emergency number is called, the sooner early advanced medical care arrives.

2. **Early CPR.** Early CPR helps circulate blood that contains oxygen to the vital organs until an automated external defibrillator (AED) is ready to use or advanced medical personnel arrive.

3. **Early defibrillation.** Most people with sudden cardiac arrest need an electric shock called defibrillation. Each minute that defibrillation is delayed reduces the chance of survival by about 10 percent.

4. **Early advanced medical care.** This is given by trained medical personnel who give further medical care and transport to hospital facilities.

In the Cardiac Chain of Survival, each link of the chain depends on and is connected to the other links. It is very important to recognize and start CPR promptly and continue it until an AED is available or EMS personnel arrive and take over. Any delay in calling 9-1-1 or the local emergency number, starting CPR and using an AED makes it less likely the person will survive. Remember, you are the first link in the Cardiac Chain of Survival.

CPR—Child and Infant

CPR—Child

Unlike adults, children (ages 1 year to 12 years) seldom initially suffer a cardiac (heart) emergency. Instead, they suffer a breathing emergency such as a severe asthma attack that leads to a cardiac emergency. Motor vehicle crashes, drowning, suffocation, poisoning, choking and fires and flames are also all common causes of breathing emergencies that can develop into a cardiac emergency.

If a child shows no signs of life (no movement or breathing) and does not have a pulse, he or she needs CPR. CPR is a combination of cycles of 30 chest compressions and 2 rescue breaths. See CPR—Child Skill Sheet, found on page 159.

CPR—Infant

A cardiac emergency in an otherwise healthy infant (newborn to 1 year) is not common unless there has been a serious injury, sudden infant death syndrome (SIDS) or a breathing emergency like choking and the infant has not been successfully revived in time. Infants who are born with problems with the heart's structure or function may have a higher risk for cardiac emergencies.

If an infant shows no signs of life (no movement or breathing) and does not have a pulse, he or she needs CPR. Infant CPR is similar to child CPR in that you give a combination of cycles of 30 chest compressions and 2 rescue breaths. See the CPR—Infant Skill Sheet, found on page 160.

AED

Sometimes cardiac arrest occurs because the person's heart rhythms are not normal, causing the heart to suddenly stop pumping blood. Most victims of sudden cardiac arrest need immediate CPR and may need an electric shock called defibrillation. AEDs are portable electronic devices that can deliver a defibrillation shock to help the heart restore an effective (pumping) rhythm. Certain AEDs with pediatric AED pads can deliver lower levels of energy considered appropriate to a child or an infant under age 8 or less than 55 pounds. An AED can deliver that shock, either automatically or with the push of a button. The greatest chance of survival from sudden cardiac arrest occurs when the four links of the Cardiac Chain of Survival happen as rapidly as possible.

CONTINUOUS CHEST COMPRESSIONS

If you are unwilling, unable or untrained to give full CPR (with rescue breaths), give continuous chest compressions after EMS personnel have been called. It is better to give chest compressions than nothing at all. Chest compressions may benefit the child or infant. Always be sure that 9-1-1 or the local emergency number has been called. Continue chest compressions until EMS personnel arrive or you find an obvious sign of life.

Unconscious Choking—Child and Infant

If you try rescue breaths but are unable to make the child's or infant's chest clearly rise, something may be blocking the airway and you must act quickly to get air into the child or infant. The care for an unconscious choking child or infant is very similar to the skill of CPR, with the exception that you look for (and remove, if seen) a foreign object between compressions and breaths. Chest compressions are used to help force air from the lungs to remove the object. See the Unconscious Choking—Child or Infant Skill Sheet, found on pages 161-162.

Injuries to Muscles, Bones and Joints

Types of Muscle, Bone and Joint Injuries

Injuries to muscles, bones and joints include fractures, dislocations, sprains and strains. A **fracture** is a complete break, chip or crack in a bone. Fractures can be open or closed. An open fracture happens when a bone is severely injured, causing the bone ends to tear through the skin and surrounding tissue. **Dislocations** are when there is movement of a bone at a joint away from the normal position. **Sprains** are the tearing of ligaments at a joint. **Strains** are the stretching and tearing of muscles or tendons.

Signals of Muscle, Bone and Joint Injuries

Always suspect a serious injury when any of the following signals are present:

- Bones or joints are clearly out of normal shape
- Bruising and swelling
- Child cannot use the affected part of the body normally
- Pieces of the bone are sticking out of a wound
- Child feels bones grating or felt or heard a snap or pop at the time of injury
- Injured area is cold and numb
- What happened makes you think the injury may be severe

Care for Muscle, Bone and Joint Injuries

It is difficult to know if a muscle, bone or joint injury is a fracture, dislocation, sprain or strain. It is not necessary to know the type of injury; the care given is the same for all four types.

If a muscle, bone or joint injury occurs, follow the care steps in the emergency reference guide for R.I.C.E., found on page 37, Open Fracture, found on page 38 or Splinting, found on page 38.

Splinting

Splinting is a way to prevent movement of an injured muscle, bone or joint and should be used ONLY if you have to move or transport a child to get medical attention AND if splinting does not cause more pain.

If you have to splint an injury:

- Splint the injury in the position in which you find it.
- For an injured joint, splint the *bones* above and below the injured joint.
- For an injured bone, splint the *joints* above and below the injured bone.
- Check for circulation (feeling, warmth and color) before and after splinting.

Methods of Splinting

- **Anatomic splints**. A part of the child's body is the splint. For example, you can splint an arm to the chest or an injured leg to the uninjured leg.
- **Soft splints**. Soft materials, such as a folded blanket, towels or pillows, or a folded triangular bandage, can be splint materials. A sling is a specific kind of soft splint that uses a triangular bandage tied to support an injured arm, wrist or hand.
- **Rigid splints**. Boards, folded magazines, newspapers, pieces of cardboard or metal strips without sharp edges can serve as rigid splints.
- **The ground**. An injured leg stretched out on the ground is splinted by the ground.

Head, Neck and Back Injuries
Signals of Head, Neck and Back Injuries

- Changes in consciousness
- Severe pain or pressure in the head, neck or back
- Tingling or loss of feeling in the hands, fingers, feet or toes
- Unable to move a body part
- Unusual bumps or depressions on the head or over the neck and back
- Blood or other fluids in the ears or nose
- Heavy external bleeding of the head, neck or back

- Seizures
- Trouble breathing or seeing as a result of the injury
- Nausea or vomiting
- Headache that will not go away
- Loss of balance
- Bruising of the head, especially around the eyes and behind the ears

When to Suspect Head, Neck or Back Injuries

You should think there might be a head, neck or back injury if the child or infant—

- Was involved in a motor vehicle crash.
- Was injured as a result of a fall from a height greater than his or her own height.
- Says there is neck or back pain.
- Has tingling or weakness in the arms or legs.
- Is not fully alert.
- Staggers when trying to walk.
- Appears to be weak.

Care for Head, Neck and Back Injuries

If you think a child or an infant has a head, neck or back injury, DO NOT move the head, neck or back. Place your hands on both sides of the child's or infant's head, keeping the head in the position you found it. For more information on how to care for head, neck and back injuries, go to pages 33-34 in the emergency reference guide.

Sudden Illness

Sudden illnesses include—

- Fainting.
- Diabetic emergency.
- Seizure.
- Poisoning.
- Allergic reaction.

Signals of Sudden Illness

When a child or an infant becomes suddenly ill, he or she usually looks and feels sick. Common signals include—

- Changes in consciousness, such as feeling light-headed or dizzy or becoming unconscious.
- Nausea or vomiting.
- Trouble speaking or slurred speech.
- Numbness or weakness.
- Loss of vision or blurred vision.
- Changes in breathing; the child or infant may have trouble breathing or may not be breathing normally.
- Changes in skin color (pale, ashen [gray] or flushed skin).
- Sweating.
- Continuous pressure or pain.
- Diarrhea.
- Seizures.
- Inability to move (paralysis).
- Severe headache.

Care for Sudden Illness

It is not necessary to know the exact illness. Just follow these steps:

- Do no further harm.
- Check the scene for clues about what might be wrong, and then check the child or infant.
- Call or have someone else call 9-1-1 or the local emergency number for life-threatening emergencies.
- Closely watch breathing and consciousness.
- Help the child or infant rest in the most comfortable position.
- Keep the child or infant from getting chilled or overheated.
- Reassure the child or infant.
- Give any specific care needed.

Sudden Illnesses

Directions: Fill in the blanks as you watch the video segment, "Sudden Illness."

1. If you know a child or an infant has a medical condition, you can give more specific care than if you did not know the cause of a sudden illness. These medical conditions could include _____, _____, _____, _____ and _____.

2. If a child or an infant vomits and is unconscious or lying down, position the child or infant on his or her _____ (this helps keep the airway open).

3. If a child or an infant faints and you do not think he or she has a head, neck or back injury, position the child or infant on his or her _____ and elevate the _____ about _____.

4. If you know that a child is diabetic and the child is conscious and showing signals of a diabetic emergency, give him or her _____.

5. If you think a child has been poisoned, and a life-threatening condition is found, call _____. Otherwise, call _____ and follow the directions.

Fainting

When a child or an infant suddenly loses consciousness and then reawakens, he or she may simply have fainted. Fainting is not usually harmful and the person will generally quickly recover. Lower the child or infant to the ground or other flat surface and place him or her on his or her back. If possible, raise the child's legs to about 12 inches. Loosen any tight clothing. Check to make sure the child or infant is breathing. Do not give the child or infant anything to eat or drink. If the child or infant vomits, position him or her on the side. For more information on how to care for fainting, go to page 46 in the emergency reference guide.

Diabetic Emergencies

Children and infants who are diabetic sometimes become ill because there is too much or too little sugar in their blood. The signals of a diabetic emergency are the same as for any other sudden illness, and they require the same care. During the family interview, parents should tell you if their children are diabetic and what to do for them in a diabetic emergency. Often diabetics know what is wrong and will ask for something with sugar in it. They may carry some form of sugar with them in case they need it.

If a child or an infant is conscious and can safely swallow food or fluids, give him or her sugar, preferably in liquid form. Most fruit juices and nondiet soft drinks have enough sugar to be effective. You can also give table sugar dissolved in a glass of water. For more information on how to care for a diabetic emergency, go to pages 31-32 in the emergency reference guide.

Seizures

Although it may be frightening to watch, you can easily help care for a child or an infant who is having a seizure. Remember that he or she cannot control the seizure. Do not try to stop the seizure. Do not hold or restrain the child or infant or put anything in his or her mouth. Care for a child or an infant who has had a seizure the same way you would for an unconscious child or infant. To protect him or her from being injured, remove nearby objects that might cause injury and protect the child's or infant's head by placing a thin cushion under it. For more information on how to care for a seizure, go to pages 42-43 in the emergency reference guide.

Poisoning

A poison is any substance that can cause injury, illness or death when it gets into the body. Poisons can enter the body by ingestion (drinking or eating the poison), inhalation (breathing the poison in), absorption (the poison enters through the skin) or injection (the poison is injected into the body). When a child or an infant is sick and you are checking the scene, look for items like open or spilled containers, medicines or plants nearby. This can give you clues that a poisoning has happened.

If you suspect that a child or an infant is showing signals of poisoning, call the National Poison Control Center (PCC) Hotline at (800) 222-1222. If the child or infant is unconscious, there is a change in the level of consciousness or if another life-threatening condition is present, call 9-1-1 or the local emergency number. For more information on how to care for poisoning, go to pages 41-42 in the emergency reference guide.

Allergic Reaction

Allergic reactions are caused by the activity of the immune system. These reactions range from mild to very severe, for instance, from a common mild reaction to poison ivy (skin irritation) to a life-threatening reaction (swelling of the airway, trouble breathing and obstructed airway). Some allergies for children and infants include bee stings, pollen, animals and some foods such as nuts, peanuts or shellfish. If you notice an unusual inflammation or rash on a child's or an infant's skin just after he or she has come into contact with a substance he or she is allergic to, the child or infant may be having an allergic reaction. For more information on how to care for an allergic reaction, go to pages 6-7 in the emergency reference guide.

Heat-Related Emergencies

There are three types of heat-related emergencies.

- **Heat cramps** are painful muscle spasms that usually occur in the legs and stomach. Heat cramps are the least severe of the heat-related emergencies.

- **Heat exhaustion** (early stage) is an early sign that the body's cooling system is becoming overwhelmed. Signals of heat exhaustion include—

  - Cool, moist, pale, ashen (gray) or flushed skin color.

  - Headache, nausea or dizziness.

- Weakness or exhaustion.
- Heavy sweating.
- **Heat stroke** (late stage) is when the body's systems are overwhelmed by heat and stop working properly. Heat stroke is a life-threatening condition. Signals of heat stroke include—
  - Red, hot, dry or moist skin.
  - Changes in level of consciousness.
  - Vomiting.

When a heat emergency occurs, follow the care steps for Heat Cramps, found on page 35, Heat Exhaustion, found on pages 35-36 or Heat Stroke, found on page 36 in the emergency reference guide.

Cold-Related Emergencies

Hypothermia

Hypothermia is when the entire body cools because it can no longer keep itself warm. The child or infant will die if not given care.

Signals of Hypothermia

- Shivering, numbness, glassy stare
- Lack of interest, weakness, impaired judgment
- Loss of consciousness

Frostbite

Frostbite is the freezing of body parts exposed to the cold. How bad it is depends on the air temperature, length of exposure and the wind. Frostbite can cause the loss of fingers, hands, arms, toes, feet and legs.

Signals of Frostbite

- Lack of feeling in an affected area
- Skin that appears waxy, cold to the touch or discolored (flushed, white, yellow or blue)

When a cold-related emergency occurs, follow the care steps for Hypothermia, found on pages 30-31 or Frostbite, found on pages 29-30 in the emergency reference guide.

CPR—Child

NOTE: Use disposable gloves and other equipment to protect against disease transmission.

CHECK the scene. **CHECK** the child.
IF NO SIGNS OF LIFE AND NO PULSE—
CALL 9-1-1.

After checking an injured or ill child—

 Give cycles of 30 chest compressions (A) and 2 rescue breaths (B).

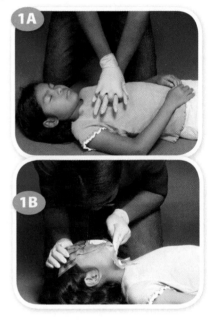

2 Continue CPR until—
- The scene becomes unsafe.
- You find a sign of life.
- You are too exhausted to continue.
- Another trained responder arrives and takes over.
- An AED is available and you are trained to use it.

WHAT TO DO NEXT
USE AN AED AS SOON AS ONE BECOMES AVAILABLE.

CPR—Infant

NOTE: Use disposable gloves and other equipment to protect against disease transmission.

CHECK the scene. **CHECK** the infant.
IF NO SIGNS OF LIFE AND NO PULSE—
CALL 9-1-1.

After checking an injured or ill infant—

 Give cycles of 30 chest compressions (A) and 2 rescue breaths (B).

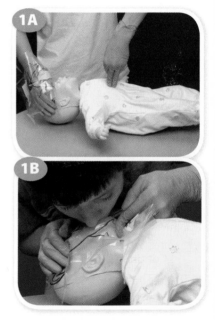

Continue CPR until—
- The scene becomes unsafe.
- You find a sign of life.
- You are too exhausted to continue.
- Another trained responder arrives and takes over.
- An AED is available and you are trained to use it.

WHAT TO DO NEXT
USE AN AED AS SOON AS ONE BECOMES AVAILABLE.

Unconscious Choking— Child or Infant

NOTE: Use disposable gloves and other equipment to protect against disease transmission.

CHECK the scene. **CHECK** the child or infant.
CALL 9-1-1.
IF FIRST 2 RESCUE BREATHS DO NOT MAKE THE CHEST CLEARLY RISE—

 Retilt the child's or infant's head.
Try 2 rescue breaths again.

If chest still does not rise—
- Give 30 chest compressions

NOTE: Remove breathing barrier when giving chest compressions.

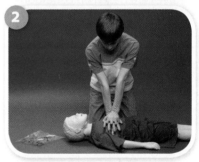

Look for an object.

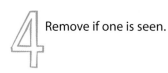 Remove if one is seen.

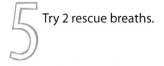 Try 2 rescue breaths.

WHAT TO DO NEXT

IF BREATHS DO NOT GO IN—Continue Steps 2–5.

IF BREATHS GO IN—

○ Check for signs of life and a pulse.

○ Give care based on conditions found.

Applying a Soft Splint

NOTE: Use disposable gloves and other equipment to protect against disease transmission.

CHECK the scene. **CHECK** the child or infant.
CALL 9-1-1 if necessary.

1 Support the injured area above and below the site of the injury.

2 Check for feeling, warmth and color.

3 Place several folded triangular bandages above and below the injured area.

4 Gently wrap a soft object (a folded blanket or pillow) around the injured area.

5 Tie triangular bandages securely.

6 Recheck for feeling, warmth and color.

NOTE: *If you are not able to check warmth and color because a sock or shoe is in place, check for feeling.*

Applying a Sling and Binder

NOTE: Use disposable gloves and other equipment to protect against disease transmission.

CHECK the scene. **CHECK** the child or infant. **CALL** 9-1-1 if necessary.

1 Support the injured area above and below the site of the injury.

2 Check for feeling, warmth and color.

3 Place one end of a triangular bandage under the injured arm and over the uninjured shoulder to form a sling.

4 Tie the ends of the sling at the side of the neck.

5 Bind the injured area to the chest with a folded triangular bandage.

6 Recheck for feeling, warmth and color.

References

2005 International Consensus on CPR and ECC Science with Treatment Recommendations Guidelines 2005 for First Aid. *Circulation* 2005;112 (Issue 22): Supplement.

About.com. http://childcare.about.com.

Alberta Municipal Affairs and Housing. *Babysitter's Guide to Fire Safety—Canada.* www.municipalaffairs.gov.ab.ca/fco/pdf/babysitter.pdf.

American Academy of Child and Adolescent Psychiatry. http://www.aacap.org.

American Academy of Pediatrics. http://www.aap.org/.

American Academy of Pediatric Dentistry. http://www.aapd.org.

American Heart Association and the American National Red Cross, 2005 *Guidelines for First Aid,* Supplement to *Circulation.* http://www.circulationaha.org.

American Library Association. www.ala.org.

American Red Cross. 2006. *First Aid for Schools and the Community.* Yardley, PA: StayWell.

American Red Cross. 2002. *First Aid Fast.* Washington. D.C.: StayWell.

American Red Cross. 2002. *First Aid for Children Today.* Washington, D.C.: StayWell.

AskDrSears.com. http://askdrsears.com.

Babysittingclass.com. http://www.babysittingclass.com.

Biting—Parenting. http://missourifamilies.org/FEATURES/parentingarticles/parenting1.htm.

Calgary Police Service. *Kids & Teens.* www.calgarypolice.ca/kids/babysitting.html.

Centers for Disease Control and Prevention. *Facts About Lyme Disease.* http://www.cdc.gov/od/oc/media/fac/lyme.htm.

Centers for Disease Control and Prevention, National Center for Injury Prevention and Control. *Scientific Data, Surveillance, and Injury Statistics.* http://www.cdc.gov/ncipc/osp.data.htm.

Center for Effective Parenting. http://www.parenting-ed.org.

Child Trends. http://www.childtrends.org/.

CYFERnet. www.cyfernet.org.

Dakota County Attorney's Office. http://www.co.dakota.mn.us/Departments/Attorney/FAQ/WhatAgeChildLeftHomeAloneHowLong.htm.

Department of the U.S. Army. *Hooah4health.* http://www.hooah4health.com.

Epilepsy Foundation of America. *Epilepsy: A Report to the Nation.* http://www.efa.org/epusa/nation/nation.html.

High Beam Encyclopedia. *Desert Survival.* www.encyclopedia.com/doc/1G1-111979685.html.

4Homehelp.com. http://www.4homehelp.com.

Jeffrey H.S., Megevand A., and Page H.D. as quoted by Sudden Death Syndrome Network. http://www.sids-network.org/experts/prone-risk.html.

Johnson D.W., and Johnson F. P. 2003. *Joining Together: Group Theory and Group Skills.* Boston: Allyn & Bacon.

Johnson D.W., and Johnson R.T. 1997. *Learning to Lead Teams: Developing Leadership Skills.* Edina, MN: Interaction Book Company.

Johnson D.W., Johnson R.T., and Holubec E.J. 1998. *Cooperation in the Classroom (Revised).* Edina, MN: Interaction Book Company.

Kentucky Governor's Office of Constituent Services. http://constituentservices. ky.gov.

Kids Health. www.KidsHealth.org.

Kids Health. *What is Hyperactivity?* www.KidsHealth.org.

Latane B., and Darley J.M. 1970. *The Unresponsive Bystander: Why Doesn't He Help?* New York: Appleton-Century-Crofts.

Litovitz T.L, Klein-Schwartz W, Caravati E.M., Youniss J., Crouch B., and Lee S. 1998 Annual Report of the American Association of Poison Control Centers Toxic Exposure Surveillance System. *American Journal of Emergency Medicine* 1999;17(5): 435–487.

Magellan Health Services. https://www.magellanassist.com.

Maryland Department of Juvenile Services. http://www.djs.state.md.us/faq.html.

McGruff the Crime Dog. www.mcgruff-tid.com.

MedlinePlus. http://medlineplus.gov.

National Child Care Information Center. www.nccic.org/.

National Crime Prevention Council. www.ncpc.org/.

National Fire Protection Association. *NFPA Fact Sheet on Home Fire Statistics.* http://www.nfpa.org.

National Heart, Lung and Blood Institute, National Institutes of Health. http://nhlbi.nih.gov.

National Institute of Mental Health. 1994. *Attention Deficit Hyperactivity Disorder.* Bethesda, MD: National Institute of Mental Health, National Institutes of Health, U.S. Department of Health and Human Services.

National Maternal Child Health Clearinghouse. http://www.nmchc.org.

National Network for Child Care. www.nncc.org/.

Norman M., and Munson M.K. 1992. Leadership Skills You Never Outgrow. In *Leadership Project Book II: Individual Skills for Older Members.* Champaign, IL: University of Illinois Cooperative Extension Service.

North Carolina Cooperative Extension Service. *Childhood Aggression: Where Does it Come From? How Can it be Managed?* http://www.ces.ncsu.edu/depts/ fcs/human/pubs/aggression.html.

Palm Beach Herpetological Society in Cooperation with the Florida Cooperative Extension Service, Institute of Food and Agricultural Sciences, University of Florida. *Venomous Snake Bite.* http://www.cdc.gov.niosh/nasd/docs/as31600. html.

PBS. http://pbskids.org/license.

Regents of the University of Minnesota. *How to Guide a Child's Misbehavior, #706.* http://www.extension.umn.edu/info-u/families/BE706.html.

Safe Kids USA. www.usa.safekids.org/.

Students Against Destructive Decisions. www.saddonline.com.

Sudden Infant Death Syndrome Alliance. *Facts About Sudden Infant Death Syndrome.* http://www.sidsalliance.org.

Texas Cooperative Extension, Texas A & M University System. http://texasextension.tamu.edu.

University of Florida. *UF/IFAS Extension Solutions for Your Life.* http://solutionsforyourlife.ufl.edu/.

University of Illinois Extension. *A Guide to the Business of Babysitting.* http://www.urbanext.uiuc.edu/babysitting/safety.html.

University of Kentucky. *America at War: Helping Children Cope.* http://www.ca.uky.edu/fcs/AmericaAtWar/article1.htm.

University of Maine. *Growing Ideas: Ouch! That Hurts—Biting.* http://www.ccids.umaine.edu/ec/growingideas/bitinglg.pdf.

University of Michigan. *Pediatric Advisor 2006. Dealing with Attention-Deficit-Hyperactivity Disorder (ADHD).* www.med.umich.edu/1libr/pa/pa_battentn_hhg.htm.

University of Michigan Health System. http://www.med.umich.edu.

University of Minnesota Center for Early Education and Development. *Tip Sheets.* http://cehd.umn.edu/ceed/publications/tipsheets/default.html.

U.S. Consumer Product Safety Commission. www.cpsc.gov.

U.S. Department of Defense. http://www.defenselink.mil.

U.S. Department of Education. *Healthy Start Grow Smart Series 2002.* http://www.ed.gov/parents/earlychild/ready/healthystart/index.html.

U.S. Department of Health and Human Services, Centers for Disease Control and Prevention. www.cdc.gov.

U.S. Environmental Protection Agency. *Sunwise Program.* http://www.epa.gov/sunwise/.

U.S. Fire Administration. *Fire Safety Information FACTSHEETS.* http://www.fire.nist.gov/factsheets/Escape.pdf.

World Kids Network. http://www.worldkids.net.

Youth Online Club. http://www.youthonline.ca/safety/kitchensafety.shtml.

Zero to Three. www.zerotothree.org.

About the American Red Cross